T0328554

Regional Economic Communities

This book is a product of the CODESRIA
13th General Assembly, 2011

Africa and the Challenges of the Twenty-first Century

Regional Economic Communities

Exploring the Process of Socio-economic
Integration in Africa

Edited by

Akinpelu O. Olutayo
Adebusuyi I. Adeniran

CODESRIA

Council for the Development of Social Science Research in Africa
DAKAR

© CODESRIA 2015

Council for the Development of Social Science Research in Africa
Avenue Cheikh Anta Diop, Angle Canal IV
BP 3304 Dakar, 18524, Senegal
Website: www.codesria.org

ISBN: 978-2-86978-632-5

Typesetting: Sériane Camara Ajavon

Cover Design: Ibrahima Fofana

Distributed in Africa by CODESRIA

Distributed elsewhere by African Books Collective, Oxford, UK.
Website: www.africanbookscollective.com

The Council for the Development of Social Science Research in Africa (CODESRIA) is an independent organisation whose principal objectives are to facilitate research, promote research-based publishing and create multiple forums geared towards the exchange of views and information among African researchers. All these are aimed at reducing the fragmentation of research in the continent through the creation of thematic research networks that cut across linguistic and regional boundaries.

CODESRIA publishes *Africa Development*, the longest standing Africa based social science journal; *Afrika Zamani*, a journal of history; the *African Sociological Review*; the *African Journal of International Affairs*; *Africa Review of Books* and the *Journal of Higher Education in Africa*. The Council also co-publishes the *Africa Media Review*; *Identity, Culture and Politics: An Afro-Asian Dialogue*; *The African Anthropologist* and the *Afro-Arab Selections for Social Sciences*. The results of its research and other activities are also disseminated through its Working Paper Series, Green Book Series, Monograph Series, Book Series, Policy Briefs and the CODESRIA Bulletin. Select CODESRIA publications are also accessible online at www.codesria.org.

CODESRIA would like to express its gratitude to the Swedish International Development Cooperation Agency (SIDA), the International Development Research Centre (IDRC), the Ford Foundation, the Carnegie Corporation of New York (CCNY), the Norwegian Agency for Development Cooperation (NORAD), the Danish Agency for International Development (DANIDA), the French Ministry of Cooperation, the United Nations Development Programme (UNDP), the Netherlands Ministry of Foreign Affairs, the Rockefeller Foundation, the Open Society Foundations (OSFs), Trust Africa, UNESCO, UN Women, the African Capacity Building Foundation (ACBF) and the Government of Senegal for supporting its research, training and publication programmes.

Contents

Contributors

Terfa Williams Abraham obtained his BSc and MSc degrees in Economics from the Ahmadu Bello University, Zaria-Nigeria and a Certificate in Economics of Climate Change from the AERC/UNU-WIDER training in Cape Town, South Africa. An Associate Member of the Nigerian Economic Society (NES) and Individual Member of CODESRIA, his research interests are in Financial Markets, Public Finance, Climate Change and Development Economics. He is currently a Research Officer at the National Institute for Legislative Studies (NILS), National Assembly, Abuja, Nigeria.

Adebusuyi Isaac Adeniran is a Lecturer/Researcher in Sociology at the Obafemi Awolowo University, Nigeria and a visiting researcher at The Harriet Tubman Institute, York University, Canada. He holds a PhD in Development Sociology from the University of Ibadan, Nigeria. He has published in widely acclaimed local and international journals, periodicals, books and encyclopaedias. His recent articles explain the usefulness of an endogenous development framework in West Africa (*Critical Sociology*, Sage, 2012) and the dynamics of cross-border relation in the ECOWAS sub-region (Blackwell, 2013). He is a recipient of the Africa Initiative Graduate Research Grant (Canada 2011) and CODESRIA's Comparative Research Network Grant (2012) among other scholarly awards.

Olayinka Akanle is a Lecturer at the Department of Sociology, Faculty of the Social Sciences, University of Ibadan, Nigeria. He has published extensively in books, encyclopaedias and learned journals, both locally and internationally, including; Akanle, O. and Olutayo, A.O., 2012, 'Ethnography of Kinship Constructions among International Returnees in Nigeria: Proverbs as the Horses of Words', *Journal of Anthropological Research*. 68.2; Olutayo, A.O and Akanle, O., 2009, 'Fast Foods in Ibadan Metropolis: An Emerging Consumption Pattern', *Africa*, 79.2, pp. 207-227.

Kabran Aristide Djane is a Lecturer/Researcher at the Department of Sociology and Anthropology, University of Korhogo, Ivory Coast. He is a specialist in population and development studies. He focuses his research on African fieldworks by applying modelling in social sciences. He has modelled children's environmental behaviour in many of his research works. He is currently working on multilevel analysis in children agencies.

Leah Kimathi holds a Masters degree in History of International Relations from Kenyatta University and a Fellowship in International Philanthropy from Johns Hopkins University, USA. She has published extensively on peace and security, post-conflict recovery as well as the role of non-formal institutions in peace building. A recipient of many academic and social activism awards, she is currently working with the UNDP Somalia as a Community Safety Specialist.

Ikuteyijo Lanre Olusegun is a Lecturer in the Department of Sociology and Anthropology, Obafemi Awolowo University, Ile-Ife, Nigeria. He specialised in Criminology and Social Research Methods from Obafemi Awolowo University, Ile-Ife. His research interests include policing, migration, urbanisation and social research methods. He was a visiting researcher to McMaster University, Hamilton, Canada in 2011 and 2012. He is a recipient of a number of awards including the 'Network of Excellence for Qualitative Research in the Social Sciences: Sub-Saharan Africa'.

Akinpelu Olanrewaju Olutayo is a Professor of Sociology at the University of Ibadan, Nigeria and a visiting lecturer to the University of Ghana, Ghana, University of Botswana, Botswana, Olabisi Onabanjo University, Nigeria and Obafemi Awolowo University, Nigeria. He is an external examiner at various universities in Nigeria and overseas. He has published more than 50 research papers in established local and international journals. He has also written and edited more than 10 publications.

Molatokunbo Oluwaseunfunmi Olutayo holds a PhD in Political Science from University of Ibadan, Nigeria. She specializes in gender and political life. She has previously served as a lecturer at the Olabisi Onabanjo University, Nigeria and Lead City University, Nigeria. She is currently a Faculty Member at the Institute of African Studies, University of Ibadan, Nigeria. She has published well-researched articles in notable local and international journals.

Ayokunle Olumuyiwa Omobowale teaches Sociology at the University of Ibadan. He holds a PhD. degree in Sociology. He was a recipient of the 2010 American Council of Learned Societies African Humanities Programme Post-Doctoral Fellowship among other scholarly awards. He has published in reputable journals and edited volumes both locally and internationally. He has interest in Sociology of Development, Urban Sociology, Rural Sociology and Sociological Theory. He is the author of *The Tokunbo Phenomenon and the Second-Hand Economy in Nigeria* (2013).

Bappah Habibu Yaya is a Lecturer in the Department of Political Science, Faculty of Social Sciences, Ahmadu Bello University, Zaria. He holds a BSc. degree in International Studies and an MSc degree in Political Science from Ahmadu Bello University, Zaria. He is currently at the completion stage of his PhD. His research interest is in Regional Integration in Africa, particularly the Economic Community of West African States (ECOWAS).

Benaiah Yongo-Bure is Associate Professor of Social Science. He teaches Economics and Social Science at Kettering University, Flint, Michigan. Yongo obtained his MA and PhD degrees from Dalhousie University, Canada, after graduating with a BA. (Hons) from Makerere University, Uganda. Before joining Kettering, Yongo had taught Economics at the University of Khartoum, University of Juba and Wayne State University, Detroit. Yongo's research interests are in African development, regional integration and peace and conflict issues.

Olabisi S. Yusuff is a Lecturer in Sociology at the Lagos State University, Nigeria. She is currently working at completing her doctoral research at the Department of Sociology, University of Ibadan, Nigeria. She has researched and published locally and internationally on subjects related to gender and development.

Introduction

Akinpelu O. Olutayo and Adebusuyi I. Adeniran

The unprecedented speed at which change occurs in different countries and in all aspects of people's lives over the last two decades; has made it imperative to revisit the erection of any kind of barriers across countries' borders. Viewed in the context of ideological, economic, technological or developmental perspectives, there has been increasing inter-societal, or better still, inter-regional competiveness across vast geographical spaces. This has brought about a need for capacity strengthening beyond respective nationalistic frameworks, and more significantly at the level of economic functioning in order to strengthen the competitive advantage of participating member-states (Adeniran 2012:2). Against this background, Regional Economic Communities (RECs) in Africa are described as imperative platforms for grouping individual countries together within different sub-regions for the specific objectives of attaining greater socio-economic unification.

Ostensibly, the logic underlying the institutionalization of the RECs in Africa has been to engender enhanced group competitiveness within the global economic framework; hence the wide range of regional institutions in place. While the african Union (AU) stands at the apex of African socio-economic and political cooperation, at the sub-regional level, Africa's RECs comprise various groups of neighbouring countries working together to address common developmental concerns, such as enabling free movement of persons and goods, and essentially working towards attaining political unification (World Bank 2011). While numerous RECs exist in Africa, only eight are officially recognized by the AU: the Arab Maghreb Union (UMA), the Common Market for Eastern and Southern Africa (COMESA), the Community of Sahel and Saharan States (CEN-SAD), the East African Community (EAC), the Economic Community of Central African States, (ECCAS), the Economic Community of West African States (ECOWAS), the Intergovernmental Authority on Development (IGAD) and the Southern Africa Development Community (SADC). These RECs are generally projected (and meant) to serve as imperative 'building blocks' to the target of the 'African common market' and are considered central to the realization of the goals of the New Partnership for Africa's Development (NEPAD).

Depending on the focus and goals of participating nation-states, regional integration could entail economic, cultural, political and military (including trans-border security) unification/cooperation; which translates to 'deep integration'. If a specific regional integration project focuses on an all-encompassing framework, then 'deep integration' is advanced. As a matter of routine, deep integration obliterates the position of 'methodological nationalism', since the significance of any defined borders of the participating nation-states is demystified. Since most efforts targeted at regional unification in parts of Africa have been programmatically patterned after the European Union (EU) model, the idea of a holistic 'deep integration' has been of less concern. Rather, economic (as well as monetary) integration has been focused on, just as it exists in the subsisting EU framework. Consequently, various RECs projects in Africa have not been immune from extant challenges faced by the EU experimentation some of which show in the recent threat by the United Kingdom to pull out of the EU (through a referendum being planned for 2015) due to perceived unfair treatment by 'economically bigger participants' – Germany and France.

Within the interactive framework of various RECs in Africa, intra-regional suspicion and competition among member-states has been hindering the attainment of extant regional socio-economic goals, just as it is being reflected in the relationship of Britain with the European Union. Besides, the continued cleavage of many African countries to their former colonial masters has been antithetical to the positions of the RECs in Africa. For instance, within the West African sub-region, such cleavage has been responsible for the prioritization of national (and subsisting colonial) interests to the detriment of any (sub) regional agenda. Interestingly, within the ECOWAS configuration, eight monetary zones are currently in place. Such development has not augured well for successful implementation of relevant frameworks of various RECs within the sub-region.

The existence of overlapping institutions within various sub-regions in Africa has presented a daunting challenge to the workings of the RECs on the continent. The majority of the African countries are members of overlapping and, sometimes, contradictory RECs. For instance, in East Africa, while Kenya and Uganda are both members of EAC and COMESA, Tanzania, which is also a member of the EAC, left COMESA in 2001 to join SADC. In West Africa, while all former French colonies, such as Mali, Cote d'Ivoire, Togo and Benin Republic belong to the ECOWAS, they simultaneously keep membership of the West African Economic and Monetary Union (UEMOA), though unrecognized by the AU. Such multiple and confusing membership creates unnecessary duplication and dims the light on what ought to be priority.

Various chapters in this book have therefore sought to identify and proffer solutions to related challenges confronting the workings of the RECs in parts of the African continent. The discourses range from security to the stock exchange, identity integration, development framework, labour movement and cross-border relations. The pattern adopted in the project engages devolution of related discussions from the general to the specific; that is from larger African configuration to sub-regional case studies. Owing to the popularity of ongoing intent of the ECOWAS authorities to transmute the West African sub-region from 'ECOWAS of States to ECOWAS of People', in which the goal of a borderless sub-region will be attained, most of the specific case studies in this publication emanated from the ECOWAS sub-region.

Chapter 1 identifies 'multiple regionalisms' in Africa as the primary albatross of the regional integration project of the continent. The existence of several sub-regional groupings, whose objectives and programmes, in many instances, are contradictory, has been complicating the processes of integration in the continent. Multiple memberships of different regional groupings by most African countries have made the expected impacts of various RECs ineffective in Africa. Overlapping sub-regional groupings have facilitated operational problems in governance and administration of the African integration project. On the one hand, there has been the challenge of dispersal of scarce diplomatic, economic and human resources, especially among mostly poor member states. On the other hand, multiple sub-regional groupings have engendered excessive politicization of the African integration effort. Effective regional governance for integration is hindered by ingrained disagreements among leading member-states within various sub-regional groupings. On the whole, the performance of these sub-regional groupings has been dismal and, of course, antithetical to their envisaged roles as imperative building blocks for larger African socio-economic integration (ARIA 2002). This chapter unequivocally affirms 'inter-regionalism' (that is, the institutionalization of interactions among various sub-regional groupings) as the framework that could assist in overcoming the challenges of multiple regionalism, and help in accelerating the socio-economic integration of Africa.

Chapter 2 concentrates on how Regional Development Poles (RDPs) could be engaged as potent strategies for attaining socio-economic transformation of Africa. The idea focuses on using a few large African countries, which could industrialize on their own, given their huge natural and human resources as well as their large domestic markets, in the process of transforming Africa to modernity. From the RDPs, faster economic development will diffuse to other surrounding smaller African nation-states. The diffusion will be accelerated by establishing inter-African infrastructural networks. At present, negligible fragmented markets of most African economies cannot support the establishment of capital goods industries. Unless established on regional basis, such industries would be underutilized in most African countries due to their relative small sizes. The chapter argues that effective regional integration in Africa would require various African countries to pool their markets and resources.

Chapter 3 explains the usefulness of the African Union's African Peace and Security Architecture (APSA) in ensuring the regional unification of Africa's security apparatus. APSA is basically designed to respond holistically to peace and security concerns on the African continent through conflict prevention, management and post-conflict peace-building. This chapter suggests that although APSA is a commendable and laudable effort by Africa to provide 'African solutions to African problems', there still subsists a number of questions regarding its sustainability and ownership. The bedrock of the architecture is daunting since various international interests have been unduly represented in the functioning of APSA and such interests have been setting the agenda for its operations.

The enabling of integration of the African continent through the platforms of harmonized sub-regional monetary and economic systems is the focus of Chapter 4. In order to achieve stronger socio-economic unification of Africa, the harmonization of varying macro-economic policies of member-states of specific RECs is deemed essential. In relation to the financial market situations, integration is adjudged as the process of unifying markets and engendering convergence of risk adjusted returns on the assets of similar maturity across the markets (Harris 2008). Besides enhancing domestic savings, and improving the probability of pricing and availability of capital for domestic utilization, integration of stock markets within the sub-regional configuration is capable of increasing the exposure of member states to increased vulnerability, which could hamper desired benefits from integration. This chapter, therefore, affirms that in extracting benefits accruable from the harmonization of the stock markets for utilization by the RECs in Africa, potent regulatory mechanisms should be advanced to mitigate the impacts of probable external shocks on member states.

Chapter 5 examines the gender dimensions of the socio-economic unification project in Africa, engaging extant cross-border trading practice in the West African sub-region as a case study. Through a qualitative research process, the author finds that a significant number of women in cross-border trading in West Africa are routinely exposed to varying degrees of insecurity posed by the informalities entailed in the trading processes. Such insecurities, which are associated with activities of law-enforcement agents and cross-border touts, have been inimical to the goal of socio-economic integration of the sub-region, and have been unproductive with regard to the realization of various programmes of the sub-regional RECs, being represented in the ECOWAS frameworks on sub-regional integration and development. The chapter advances the view that informal economic activities of women in cross-border trading in Africa should be recognized in order to have a holistic policy towards women empowerment across parts of the continent.

Chapter 6 addresses the relevance of cross-border networking process to the attainment of identity integration in Africa, using the West African sub-region as a case study. The chapter engages both historical and qualitative approaches in the process of contextualizing its objectives. Besides the economic and political focus of various REC projects in Africa, it is argued that the patterns of identity interpositions prevalent among Africans should be progressively analysed. Ongoing informal migration within the ECOWAS sub-region, for instance, has presented a formidable framework towards the realization of various integrative and developmental goals as espoused by related sub-regional frameworks. Although colonial economic policies within the emergent West African nation-states promoted an export-based economy and movement from various hinterlands to the emerging urban settlements, they indirectly discouraged cross-border interactions, especially along the Anglophone/Francophone dichotomy. Such dichotomy was to play a significant role in the formation of national outlooks for such emergent political entities in West Africa. On the one hand, the French took over some of the political entities, imposing their cultural disposition on the citizens in the disguise of 'assimilation'. On the other, although the British presented a rather cooperative mode of relationship with their African colonies in the name of 'association', they tended to affirm a distinct political identity for the colonies through the 'Commonwealth of Nations'. These developments could be readily affirmed to be the conceptual impetus for related, contemporary identity misinterpretations among the people. Yet, though ironically, such colonial creations could not stop the people from sustaining their pre-colonial socio-economic interactive patterns in the post-colonial period. Ostensibly, it would have seemed logical for the subjects of two former British colonies to be intermingling, and for the citizens of two former French colonies to be interacting. Rather, the established pre-colonial mode of interaction has outwitted the contemporary nationalistic configuration in such cases.

The menace of child labour in Africa is the focus of Chapter 7. The chapter specifically explores the process of decision-making regarding the entrance of children into the labour market in West Africa. It observes that child labour is economically built around various production areas in agricultural and urban centres in West Africa. Various agricultural regions saw the emergence of child labourers during the boom period of the 1930s (that is, the production of coffee and cocoa). It identifies both Ghana and Côte d'Ivoire as the major countries of concentration of migrant child labourers within the sub-region. Such migrant child labourers either come with their parents or on their own for work. A specific multiplier effect of this development is that courtesy of related intermingling of migrant children and the indigenous children, over time and space, cultural boundaries are becoming obliterated. As such regional integration is being enhanced.

Chapter 8 analyses how trans-border banditry could inhibit integration at the level of RECs functioning in Africa, with specific emphasis on the ECOWAS sub-region. While Africans consider regional integration a noble objective, trans-border banditry poses a huge threat to security and the integration efforts within the frameworks of various RECs in Africa.

Chapter 9 of this book examines the development model upon which the imperatives of the Structural Adjustment Programme (SAP) were situated in Africa. The implications of such imperatives for the realization of the goals of various RECs in Africa, West Africa especially, were focused on. Drawing on the lessons from the trajectories of SAP in sub-Saharan Africa, the chapter argues that Africa should take its destiny in its hands. The intended unification of the socio-economic and political system of the African continent through the workings of various RECs should be internally propelled. This would answer the need to have a sustainable framework to drive larger developmental project of the African continent.

Chapter 10 analyses the relationship between policing irregular migration and socio-economic integration in Africa. It affirms that within the West African sub-region, rising political and economic instability has produced specific attendant developments, particularly in terms of changing migration configurations. The quest for regional integration within the sub-region, therefore faces the problem of irregular and other forms of clandestine migration, which in most cases have economic and security implications. This chapter discusses the challenges of emerging problems of terrorism, economic and political instability in West Africa and the need to provide effective policing for the sub-region. Using secondary data, the chapter examines issues such as cross-border crimes, the borderless ECOWAS pact and its implications for internal security, human trafficking, child labour and organized criminal networks; information sharing, policing cooperation and illegal border tariffs as challenges to the regional integration plans for the West African sub-region. The chapter concludes by suggesting practical steps towards addressing these challenges in order to properly harness the gains of regional integration in the mode of the European Union.

References

Adeniran, A.I., 2012, 'Regional Integration in the ECOWAS Region: Challenges and Opportunities', Africa Portal, Backgrounder 19, January.

ARIA, 2002, 'Annual Report on Integration in Africa (ARIA-2002)', www.uneca.org (accessed on 12/03/2011)

World Bank, 2011, 'Regional Integration in Africa', www.worldbank.org (accessed on 27/01/2013)

Harris, L., 2008, 'Regional Integration and Capital Markets in Africa', in N. Mthuli, ed., *African Economic Research Consortium (AERC) in Financial Systems and Monetary Policy in Africa*, AERC, pp. 89-101.

1

Inter-regionalism as a Mechanism for the Harmonization of Africa's Regional Integration Projects

Bappah Habibu Yaya

Introduction

'Multiple regionalisms' are a problem in Africa's integration process. It refers to the existence of several sub-regional groupings whose objectives and programmes in many instances conflict, thereby complicating the processes of integration on the continent. Most countries in Africa hold membership in at least two different regional groupings (ARIA 2002). There are currently fourteen regional groupings in Africa, with eight recognized by the United Nations Economic Commission for Africa (UNECA) and the African Union (AU) as the building blocks of the African Economic Community (AEC). These recognized groupings are collectively referred to as regional economic communities (RECs). They are: the Arab Maghreb Union (AMU); the Economic Community of Central African States (ECCAS); the Common Market of Eastern and Southern Africa (COMESA); the East African Community (EAC); the Southern African Development Community (SADC); the Community of Sahel-Saharan States (CEN-SAD); the Intergovernmental Authority on Drought and Development (IGADD); and the Economic Community of West African States (ECOWAS) (Tadesse 2009). The others, such as the West African Economic and Monetary Union (WAEMU) and the Indian Ocean Commission (OIC) exist alongside, and compete with, the recognized regional groups on the continent. The multiplicity of these sub-regional groupings has caused operational problems in the governance and administration of the African integration processes. There is, firstly, the issue of dispersal of scarce diplomatic, economic and human resources. The mostly poor member states have had to contend with making commitments to these organizations. Secondly, the multiplicity of the groupings has created an environment for high politicization of the African integration process. Effective regional governance for integration is hampered by clashes between leading members within the different regional groupings. On the whole, the performance of these regional groupings has been dismal (ARIA 2002). Thus, this paper argues that *inter-regionalism*, i.e., the institutionalization of relations between regional groupings, is a mechanism that can help overcome the challenges of multiple regionalisms, and accelerate the integration of the continent. A case has been made by the ECA for rationalization of the regional groupings in Africa; and some principles were outlined as a general framework for dealing with multiple regionalisms in Africa (ECA 2006). These efforts, however, lack any theoretical and methodological support. *Inter-regionalism*, offers both a theoretical framework and a methodological support for overcoming the challenges of multiple regionalism in Africa. But before we explore that, it is important to begin with an examination of the concept as expounded by scholars.

Inter-regionalism: A New Dimension of Global Governance

The international system is a galaxy of multiple levels of decision-making, all of which have a bearing on states. Decision-making takes place across different strata of human organization, that is local, national, sub-regional, regional, inter-regional and global levels. Among these levels, the inter-regional level is fairly recent and has enjoyed less academic expositions. However, this level of governance is developing across different regions. Its importance is in filling the gap in governance on issues which are clearly outside the exclusive purview of sub-regional or regional authorities and beyond the capacity of multilateral institutions to handle.

The concept of *inter-regionalism* was developed to describe the institutionalization of relations between world regions (Hänggi, Rollof and Rüland 2006). It is a new structure of governance, developed to manage the manifold challenges caused by the growing incongruence between the border-crossing nature of policy matters and territorially-defined political authority (Rüland 2002:1). The transcending nature of policy matters beyond limits imposed by territoriality of political authority necessitates collaboration between regions to manage their common affairs. Just as the limits imposed by territoriality and sovereignty make states incapable of self-fulfillment and self-sustenance, and compel them to enter into relations with one another, so also do regions seek to interrelate to overcome their inadequacies.

The concept of *inter-regionalism* was developed to explain the proliferation of, and interactions between, regional groupings across the globe (Hänggi 2000). The emergence and proliferation of regional groupings in the post-cold war era created an anxiety that such regional groupings may constitute closed entities, thereby hampering global free trade and investment. That, however, did not happen as regional groups opened up to each other and engaged in mutual interactions. This is what came to be referred to as 'open regionalism', which is a policy matter concerning how to achieve compatibility between the explosion of regional trading arrangements around the world and the global trading system as embodied in the World Trade Organization (WTO) (Bergsten 2010). The concept of open regionalism assures that regional arrangements will, in practice, be building blocks for further global liberalization rather than stumbling blocks that deter such progress (Bergsten 2010). The debate about the role of regional groupings in global economy was, therefore, put to the test with the emergence of this new form of relations, *inter-regionalism*. Thus, *inter-regionalism* evolved among regional groupings as a means of managing relations among them in the post-Cold War period.

Interregional relations, generally, involve regional groupings interacting on the bases of more or less regular high-level meetings and engaging in the implementation of a number of joint projects or programmes (Hänggi 2000:4). It may also involve sharing or exchange of information and cooperation in specific issue-areas, usually in the economic sphere such as in trade and investment. In some cases a political dimention could be added to such interactions, two common examples being human rights and democracy. This is especially true with the EU's discussions on such values as human rights and fundamental freedoms with other regional groupings (Hänggi 2000). A common feature of international politics today is the discussion of many issues of national and international concern on regional, interregional and global levels. For example, tax cuts or increases within a given country or in relation to another country are discussed at the regional level. This is because most states are now involved in some forms of regional economic association. States' interests are thus aggregated within regional organizations.

Inter-regionalism has captured the attention of some scholars of international relations (Hänggi 2000; Rüland 2001 & 2002; Aggarwal and Fogarty 2003; Rollof 2006; Gilson 2005). Hänggi (2000) has developed a typology of interregional relations which identified three types: (a) relations between regional groupings; (b) bi-regional and trans-regional arrangements; and (c) hybrids, such as relations between regional groupings and the super powers. He describes relations between regions as group-to-group dialogues traditionally practised by the EU in its external relations with other regions. Examples of such relations are the EU-SADC (South Africa Development Community) dialogue partnership and the EU-Mercado Commun del Sur; while bi-regional and transnational arrangements designate the triangular structure of relations between the major three world economic regions, the Triad: North America, Western Europe and East Asia. Membership in these arrangements is more diffuse than in group-to-group dialogues. Membership is thus drawn from more than two regions, but there is some form of regional coordination. An example of bi-regional arrangement is where membership is drawn from states in two different geographic regions, such as Asia-Europe Meeting (ASEM), which includes 10 East Asian countries and the 15 member-states of the EU. Trans-regional arrangements involve membership from more than two geographical regions – for example, the Asia Pacific Economic Cooperation involving 21 Pacific Rim countries including 15 East Asian economies, three North American and two South American countries (Chile and Peru). Hybrid or relations between regional groupings and single powers denotes relations that involve a super power, whose dominant position in its own region is an equivalent of a region, such as the United States in North America, and India in

South Asia. Thus, we have EU-Russia relations, EU-India, China-Africa, etc, as examples of hybrid interregional relations (Hänggi 2000).

Hänggi's (2000) typology, however, sees region strictly in terms of geography. He posits that relations between sub-regional groupings existing in the same (geographical) region, such as the Mercosur-Andean Community link, are not considered as interregional relations (Hänggi 2000). However, region does not necessarily have to be defined territorially or geographically. A region can be seen in terms of function, where boundaries do not reflect geographical particularities, but a result of the organization of social and economic relations. Looking at function rather than geography will lead us to the opinion that the relation between such regional groupings is interregional. This is particularly so in that the notion of 'region' may be seen as a social construction of 'self' vs an 'other', which provides a basis for identification and differentiation (Gilson 2005). This conception thus enables us to adopt a broader conception of *inter-regionalism* to cover relations between regional groupings existing within the same geographical location but differentiated by the construction of self-other identity or socio-economic organization of relations between the groupings.

Systemic Functions of *Inter-regionalism*

In his study of inter-regionalism in international relations, Rüland (2002) extrapolates a number of systemic functions of *inter-regionalism*, eclectically using perspectives from neo-realism, liberal institutionalism and constructivism. These are *balancing, bandwagoning, institution-building, rationalizing, agenda-setting, stability projection* and *development promotion* (Rüland 2002:3). The balancing function of *inter-regionalism* is further classified into *power balancing and institutional balancing*. This function is based on the realist perspective of balance of power in international relations; that *inter-regionalism* serves as a means of attaining balance in power relations between nation states and, or, a group of nation states, while institutional balancing is the development of institutions to exert influence in international relations (Rüland 2002:4). *Inter-regionalism* also creates bandwagon opportunity, *bandwagoning*, where actors in international relations can get involved in ventures that will bring benefits to them. *Institution-building* is the creation of new level of policy-making in a multi-layered international system and subsidiary institutions, such as regular summits, ministerial and senior officials' rounds, business dialogues, based on the need to harmonize and develop common positions by regional groupings (Rüland 2002:5). Another function of *inter-regionalism* is *rationalizing* complex and technical interests of different actors representing diverse interests in global multilateral relations (Rüland 2002:7). For instance, through *inter-regionalism*, the Africa, Caribbean and Pacific (ACP) countries can develop a common position in their relations with the EU. *Inter-regionalism* thus serves as a clearing house for the decision-making process involving diverse groups and interests. The *agenda-setting* function of *inter-regionalism* is closely related to rationalizing. It entails identification and projection of issues for discussion in multilateral relations (Rüland 2002:8). The *identity-building* function of *inter-regionalism*, developed based on the constructivist perspective, is considered capable of fostering a sense of identity in regional groupings and thereby enhancing intra-regional integration. This is promoted by the sense or idea of self versus others, which is created in the process of inter-regionalism (Rüland 2002:8). Other aspects of the function of *inter-regionalism* identified by Rüland (2002) are *stability projection* and *development promotion*. The two functions are considered inter-related, based on the argument that economic development and prosperity are related to security. Hence, regional groupings use inter-regional relations to enhance their security by extending assistance to other regions. For instance, through a comprehensive reconstruction package for the war-torn states in the Balkans, the provision of development aid and the conclusion of free trade arrangements with southern and eastern Mediterranean countries, the EU seeks to create political stability in its immediate perimeter (Rüland 2002:9).

Although not all these functions of *inter-regionalism* are empirically determined, they are theoretically tenable. We have here further surmised another function of *inter-regionalism*, which can be added to the list of functions developed by Rüland (2002) – that is, *inter-regionalism* as a *problem-solving mechanism* to the challenges of multiplicity of regional integration projects in Africa. We argue here that it is capable of solving some of the problems associated with Africa's integration by promoting the harmonization and coordination of multiple sub-integration schemes on the continent. The problem of multiple regionalisms poses a huge challenge to the realization of the African Economic Community (AEC), which is expected to materialize by 2029.

'Multiple Regionalisms' in Africa: A Challenge to the Creation of African Economic Community (AEC)

Regionalism in Africa is a matter of strategic policy drive to fulfil the ambition of harnessing the continent's peoples and resources, and managing its developmental challenges by enhancing its prospects for growth and development. However, the continent faces a crisis of management of regional integration schemes. The African Economic Community (AEC) Treaty (also known as the Abuja Treaty), which came into force in May 1994, is the crystallization of the African leaderships' commitment to cooperation and integration in economic, social and cultural fields, as contained in the past development strategies such as the Lagos Plan of Action (1980-200) and The Final Act (1980). The Treaty provided for the AEC to be established through a gradual process, which would be achieved by coordination, harmonization and progressive integration of the activities of existing and future regional economic communities (RECs) in Africa (AEC) (AU 1991). The six-stage implementation process of the Abuja Treaty, which started in 1994, envisages the creation of the Union over a period of 34 years, i.e., by 2028, as follows: STAGE 1: Strengthening existing RECs and creating new ones where needed (5 years); STAGE 2: Stabilization of tariff and other barriers to regional trade and the strengthening of sectoral integration, particularly in the field of trade, agriculture, finance, transport and communication, industry and energy, as well as coordination and harmonization of the activities of the RECs (8 years); STAGE 3: Establishment of a free trade area and a Customs Union at the level of each REC (10 years); STAGE 4: Coordination and harmonization of tariff and non-tariff systems among RECs, with a view to establishing a Continental Customs Union (2 years); STAGE 5: Establishment of an African Common Market and the adoption of common policies (4 years) and; STAGE 6: Integration of all sectors, establishment of an African Central Bank and a single African currency, setting up of an African Economic and Monetary Union and creating and electing the first Pan-African Parliament (5 years) (AEC 2003). Although these stages are not discretely pursued and with less than 17 years to the targeted date the implementation process is fraught with some challenges. A major obstacle in the way is the existence of multiple regional groupings pursuing the similar goals of integration, often in conflict with the focal points/building blocks of the continental union. That has created multiple centres of authority demanding cooperation, support and compliance with their agenda of integration. The problem has invariably become one of regional governance, where there is absence of one strong centre for building solid blocks. A number of examples can be cited here.

In the West African context, for instance, ECOWAS and the West African Economic and Monetary Union (known by its French acronym as L'UEMOA) are two rival regional groupings competing with each other to build economic and monetary community among their members. These organizations have separate but interestingly similar organizational and governance structure. They have overlapping membership. Eight members of UEMOA (Benin, Burkina Faso, Cote d'Ivoire, Guinea-Bissau, Mali, Niger, Senegal and Togo) are also members of ECOWAS. They also have similar organs and specialized institutions: they both have Authorities of Heads of State and Government, Council of Ministers, Commissions, Parliaments and Courts of Justice. In addition they each have special agencies such as Banks, e.g., the ECOWAS Bank for Investment and Development and the UEMOA's West African Development Bank and Central Bank for West African States, and so on. This existence of myriad integration institutions has no doubt caused difficulties in the administration of the sub-region's integration process, as both ECOWAS and UEMOA pursue economic integration.

Although ECOWAS is recognized by the Economic Commission for Africa (ECA) as the building block for its wider membership coverage, the activities of UEMOA cannot be overlooked. UEMOA has surpassed ECOWAS in building a monetary union and a customs union. The eight member states of UEMOA, with the assistance of France, have an established single currency, the Franc CFA (Franc of the African Financial Community), managed by a Central Bank of West Africa (BCEAO). The UEMOA member states also have a unified external tariff regime and are working towards greater regional integration by pursuing the creation of a common market that is based on free mobility of persons, goods, services and capital. ECOWAS has not yet established a single currency, but it is working towards that. It is working towards a common market as well, with its protocol on free movement of persons, residence, and establishment at various levels of implementation by the member states. Differences in the technical application of the programmes on common market pursued by the two organizations compelled their leadership to harmonize and coordinate their policies (ECOWAS 2011). At present, the trade liberalization programmes are being harmonized. ECOWAS has adopted the UEMOA Common External Tariff (CET); it is also working towards establishing a second monetary zone, the West African Monetary Zone (WAMZ), which will later be merged with the Franc CFA Zone of the UEMOA to form an all West African currency, called the ECO.

In addition, there is crisis of representation of the region in relation to the outside world. Although ECOWAS is the recognized building block for African Economic Community, it has had to coordinate its external relations with that of UEMOA. For instance, in negotiating the Economic Partnership Agreements (EPAs) with the European Union both the ECOWAS Commission and the UEMOA Commission are involved. The process of the negotiations was complicated by the lack of clarity as to the role of the two different institutions. The two organizations needed to work on common positions, as they are on different footing on some of the matters under negotiation. For example, the ECOWAS regional economic community has had to agree to work towards adopting the UEMOA common external tariff, so that the two communities can negotiate the EPA from a common standpoint on customs duties (Mangeni 2007). The West African scenario also obtains in other sub-regions of Africa.

In the Central African sub-region, the Central African Economic and Monetary Community (CEMAC) and the Economic Community of Central African States (ECCAS) are the major contending regional organizations. Although ECCAS is recognized as the pillar of the African Economic Community (AEC) from that locus, it nevertheless faces contention from another equally influential player in the regional economic integration of the sub region, i.e. CEMAC. The two organizations have overlapping membership as well. Members of CEMAC (Chad, CAR, Congo-Brazzaville, Gabon, Equatorial Guinea and Sao Tomé and Principe) are also members of ECCAS. ECCAS has a broader membership, however, with Angola, Burundi, Cameroon, Democratic Republic of Congo, and Rwanda as members in addition to all the members of CEMAC. Some of these countries are, additionally, members of other regional economic groupings, such as the Common Market for Eastern and Southern Africa (COMESA), *Communauté Economique des Pays des Grands Lacs* (CEPGL) and the East African Community (EAC). Thus, it becomes difficult to delimit the Central African region, and to have a cohesive regional economic block for the eventual establishment of an African Economic Union (Awoumou 2008). Co-coordinating the activities of ECCAS and CEMAC is one the main issues of the integration process of Central Africa.

CEMAC, which replaced UDEAC (the Customs and Economic Union of Central Africa), Africa's oldest integration body, has outpaced ECCAS on economic and monetary integration (Awoumou 2008:113). CEMAC has established a monetary union and a customs union, while ECCAS is pursuing the same. Furthermore, CEMAC started playing a political and diplomatic role in the sub-region through its fight against transnational crime, with the CEMAC Executive Secretariat providing assistance to the Central Africa Police Chiefs Committee from its creation in April 1997; the deployment of the CEMAC Multi-National Force to the Central African Republic (CAR) – FOMUC; and, the recognition of General François Bozizé's government, which came to power through coup, in June 2003 in clear contravention of the AU's doctrine of non-recognition of any regime which overthrows a democratically-elected government (Awoumou 2008:115). Within the sub-region, therefore, CEMAC has established itself as a strong regional organization.

ECCAS, on the other hand, has popular support and recognition from its international partners as the pillar of the African Economic Community (AEC) in Central Africa. ECCAS signed the Protocol on relations between United Nations Economic Commission for Africa (UNECA) and African RECs in October 1999; and in January 2001, Resolution 55/22 on cooperation between the UN and ECCAS was adopted by the UN General Assembly (Awoumou 2008:130). In July 2002, ECCAS was granted observer status at the UN. Moreover, as a result of its recognition by the AU as the pillar of ECA, ECCAS was made a focal point for the implementation and monitoring of New Partnership for Africa's Development (NEPAD) in Central Africa; in addition, in May 2003 ECCAS received institutional support from the African Development Bank (ADB) to the tune of 2.59 million unit of account (UA) to help in building the institutional capacities of the general secretariat of ECCAS (Awoumou 2008:131). However, despite this external support enjoyed by ECCAS, CEMAC was recognized by the European Union in their regional economic partnership agreements – the EPAs. This confusion as to the real representative of Central Africa vis-à-vis other regions and the wider world has no doubt created a crisis of identity for the sub-region.

Furthermore, both ECCAS and CEMAC maintain different sub-regional organs and institutions undertaking similar responsibilities, which add to the duplications in the integration process. ECCAS has a Conference of Heads of State and Government, Council of Ministers, Secretariat General, Court of Justice, Consultative Commission (AfDevInfo 2006). Similarly, CEMAC has an Executive Secretariat, Commission, Council of Ministers, Court of Justice, Community Parliament and other related specialized agencies. Given the multiplicity of institutions, overlapping membership, which contributes to an amorphous geographical region called Central Africa, and competing regional agendas between the two leading Central African regional groupings, there is undoubtedly little prospect for the emergence of a single sub-regional building block in Central Africa for the AEC.

A similar situation also exists in southern African sub-region. Here, the South Africa Development Community (SADC) and South African Customs Union (SACU) exist irreconcilably side-by-side. They also have overlapping memberships. Five member states of SADC (Botswana, Lesotho, Namibia, South Africa and Swaziland) are also members of SACU. SACU is the oldest customs union in the world (SACU 2011). Its aim is to maintain the free interchange of goods between member countries and establish a common external tariff and excise tariff in the customs area (SACU 2011). Similarly, the goal of SADC is to further socio-economic cooperation and integration as well as political and security cooperation among its 15 member states (SADC 2011a). In terms of institutional structures, SADC and SACU have established and maintained similar organs. SADC has eight institutional bodies, namely: The Summit, comprising Heads of State and Government at the top; Organ on Politics, Defence and Security (OPDS); the Council of Ministers; the Tribunal; National Committees (SNCs); and the Secretariat. SACU has four institutional organs: the Council of Ministers; Commission; Tribunal; and a Secretariat. Therefore, within the Southern African sub-region there are 13 different institutions belonging to the two organizations that are involved in one form of integration programmes or the other. That constitutes a huge challenge to the integration of the sub-region considering the demands these institutions make on the member states.

Another dimension of the challenge posed by multiple regionalisms in the southern African integration process is that some of the member states also participate in other regional economic political and security groupings that extend beyond its geographical location. These groupings also join in the competition for the attention of the member states and therefore help in undermining the objectives of those regional groupings in the sub-region. For example, South Africa and Botswana both belong to the Southern African Customs Union; Zambia is a part of the Common Market for Eastern and Southern Africa (COMESA); and Tanzania is a member of the East African Community (EAC). Thus in an attempt to harmonize the duplications in October 2008, the leadership of SADC joined with that of COMESA and the EAC to form the African Free Trade Zone. The leaders of the three trading blocs agreed to create a single free trade zone, consisting of 26 countries with a GDP of an estimated $624bn (£382.9bn). It is hoped the African Free Trade Zone agreement would ease access to markets within the zone and end problems arising from the fact that several of the member countries belong to multiple groups (BBC 2008). With all these complications, SADC is the recognized pillar for the AEC and also the platform for negotiations of the EU-APC partnerships for the southern African region. The challenge here, as in the other sub-regional communities analysed above, is to find a workable solution to the problem of duplications and scope delimitation in the integration process of southern Africa. Here, again, *inter-regionalism* can be a panacea. Creating, expanding and deepening synergy between competing economic groupings will help in building a solid block, in that the best resources of the sub-region can be harnessed under an interregional arrangement to advance a broader vision and agenda for the sub-region.

The situation is not different in eastern Africa. The East African Community (EAC) is supposed to be the pillar of the AEC in the east African sub-region. The member states (Kenya, Uganda, Tanzania, Burundi and Rwanda) are working towards the establishment of Common Market, Monetary Union and a Political Federation of the east African States (EAC 2011). These member states are also working towards achieving similar objectives as members of the Common Market for Eastern and

Southern Africa (COMESA). COMESA's main focus is the formation of a large economic and trading unit. The EAC has seven institutions (the Summit, the Council of Ministers, the Coordinating Committee, the Sectoral Committee, the East African Court of Justice, the East African Legislative Assembly and the Secretariat) working to achieve its objectives. Similarly, the decision-making structure of COMESA has at its top the Heads of State, the Council of Ministers, 12 technical committees, and a series of advisory bodies. The duplication of programmes, overlapping memberships and multiplicity of institutions is further complicated by the presence of IGAD. Intergovernmental Authority on Development (IGAD) is another designated pillar of the AEC, with headquarters in Kenya. Established initially to overcome the issues of drought and desertification, its mandate has expanded to include Conflict Prevention, Management and Resolution and Humanitarian Affairs; Infrastructure Development (Transport and Communications); Food Security and Environment Protection. However, IGAD has collaborated with COMESA and the East African Community to divide projects among themselves so that there is no duplication and to avoid approaching the same donors with the same projects (IGDA 2011). This effort is a demonstration of ad hoc measures taken by the regional groupings in the face of multiple regionalisms.

In the north African context, the largely moribund Arab Maghreb Union (AMU) exists alongside the Community of Sahel-Saharan States (CEN SAD). Although AMU is the main pillar of the AEC, it has not been functioning effectively. The Treaty establishing the Union was signed in 1989, after two decades of efforts by the member states – Algeria, Libya, Mauritania, Morocco and Tunisia (AMU 2011). The main objectives of the AMU Treaty are to strengthen all forms of ties among member states (in order to ensure regional stability and enhance policy coordination), as well as to gradually introduce free circulation of goods, services, and factors of production among them (AMU 2011). Although the AMU has no relations with the African Economic Community (AEC), and has not yet signed the Protocol on Relations with the AEC, it has, however, been designated a pillar of the AEC. The AMU is currently dormant, but attempts are under way to revive it.

In the absence of an effective AMU, CEN SAD has become a role player in the north African sub-region. Established in February 1998, with a Secretariat office based in Tripoli, Libya, CEN SAD has among its objectives the promotion of market integration of its member states through the adoption of necessary measures to ensure – a) free movement of persons, capital and interests of nationals of member states; b) right of establishment, ownership and exercise of economic activity; c) free trade and movement of goods, commodities and services from Member States and the promotion of external trade through an investment policy in Member States (CEN SAD 2011). With the exception of Algeria, all the member states of AMU are members of CEN SAD. However, the major challenge facing CEN SAD is the overlap of its agenda with the envisioned market integration schemes of ECOWAS, ECCAS and COMESA and other trade blocs more advanced in their integration (Ncube 2009). Therefore, given the situational analysis of the regional integration groupings in the continent of Africa, there is a need to have a theoretical and methodological framework within which the problem of multiple regionalisms can be overcome. In the next section, we argue that *inter-regionalism* offers a solution to the problem of multiple regionalisms.

Inter-regionalism: A Mechanism for Resolving Multiple Regionalisms in Africa

Inter-regionalism can be seen as both an approach and a mechanism for resolving regional governance and integration problems in Africa. As an approach, it gives theoretical support for a direction, already pursued by some of the RECs in the continent, of building new levels of relationship and governance structure in order to pursue a common agenda and avoid duplications. Inter-regionalism therefore provides the theoretical support that a new governance structure can emerge between the RECs when it is evident that there are gains to be made from jointly pursuing a common agenda. Furthermore, as a mechanism, *inter-regionalism* provides a framework for the rationalization of multiple RECs in Africa. This framework will involve gradual institutionalization of relations between the RECs, through regular exchanges, establishment of joint committees or secretariat, harmonization of economic and monetary projects and programmes, mandating joint institutions to implement and monitor common projects and programmes, meetings of Chief Executives of the RECs and Heads of State and Government of the RECs. Exigencies and possibly pressures to succeed may provide impetus for further expansion and deepening of relations, invariably increasing reliance on, and expansion of authority of, these new interregional institutions.

There are a number of structures and legal frameworks already in place, which constitute a basis for *inter-regionalism* in Africa. For instance, UNECA and AU have been supporting the rationalization of the RECs on the continent. Chapter IV of the Abuja Treaty carries the commitment of the member states of the AU to strengthen the existing RECs. However, it failed to specify how that can be done. At the same time, the Protocol on Relations between the AEC and the RECs, which was signed and entered into force on 25 February 1998, provides a legal structure upon which interregional relations can be developed and strengthened. One of the objectives of the protocol on relations between the AEC and the RECs is to strengthen the existing RECs in accordance with the provisions of the Abuja Treaty; to promote the coordination and harmonization of the policies, measures, programmess and activities of RECs; and, to promote closer cooperation among the RECs (Department of Foreign Affairs, Republic of South Africa 2003). Article 15 (1) of the Protocol provides for joint programmes and closer cooperation between the RECs. It says that RECs may enter into cooperation arrangements under which they undertake joint programmes or activities or more closely coordinate their policies, measures, and programmes (AU 1998). Taking the Abuja Treaty and the Protocol, a legal-political base therefore exists for advocating *inter-regionalism* in policy circles within the states and RECs.

Further, the treaties of some of the RECs provide legal basis for furthering *inter-regionalism*. Chapter XVIII of the ECOWAS Revised Treaty on Relations between the Community and other Regional Economic Communities provides that 'the Community may enter into co-operation agreements with other regional economic communities' (ECOWAS Revised Treaty 1993:44). Similarly, the very opening of the revised treaty of UEMOA expresses the loyalty of the members to the objectives of ECOWAS (L'UEMOA 2003). Moreover, Chapter II, Article 2 of the ECOWAS Revised Treaty on Establishment and Composition carries the high contracting parties' affirmation and decision that ECOWAS 'shall ultimately be the sole economic community in the region for the purpose of economic integration and the realization of the objectives of the African Economic Community' (ECOWAS Revised Treaty 1993:4). Therefore, some structures exist for *inter-regionalism* to be pursued and advanced in order to solve the problem of multiple regionalisms in Africa.

There are some efforts on the part of some of the African RECs to pursue *inter-regionalism*. These RECs have also established some interregional structures which need to be brought forward and clearly articulated. For instance, in the West African sub-region, ECOWAS and UEMOA, based on the advice of leaders in the sub-region, signed a general agreement in 2004 to enhance the coordination and harmonization of their programmes. A joint technical secretariat entrusted with the responsibility of enhancing the coordination of their joint activities was created by the two organizations. To function effectively, the two organizations would have to cede more powers to the inter-regional secretariat (GNA 2004). This joint secretariat now serves as the centre of gravity of authority toward an inter-regional governance structure in the sub-region. This form of interregional arrangement is helping to overcome the administrative challenges related to the implementation of the community programmes in West Africa. It is also helping to pool the resources of the two organizations, and to streamline their common activities. ECOWAS/UEMOA partnership is presently building around such issue-areas as the creation of West African Common Market. In this regard, a Joint Border Post (JBP) Programme is being implemented (Sanankoua 2011). There is also the convergence of economic and financial policies, particularly the sub-region's project of establishing a single currency, the ECO, on the existing UEMOA CFA zone and the non-CFA Anglophone West African Monetary Zone. Other areas of cooperation are statistical harmonization, harmonization of sectoral policies (agriculture, transportation and energy) towards preparing one of Africa's regional building blocks (ECOWAS Bulletin 2011). The joint secretariat is facilitating the cooperation programmes and projects. It can be argued that the strong understanding between the two organizations produced the political decision to sanction the former President of Ivory Coast, Laurent Gbagbo, effective when ECOWAS directed Banque Centrale des Etats de l'Afrique de l'Ouest (BCEAO) to freeze financial deals with his regime.

Similarly, within central, southern and eastern Africa an interregional collaboration is crystallizing. The leaderships of COMESA-EAC-SADC have also realized the need to chart the course of *inter-regionalism* through the framework of a Tripartite Task

Force (SADC 2011b). The framework is aimed at addressing the problems of duplication and competition in the pursuit of regional economic integration. The Tripartite Task Force thus seeks to forge collaboration and harmonize their programmes in the area of trade, customs, civil aviation, free movement of people and infrastructure development. The efforts of the Task Force saw the draft of a Tripartite Free Trade Area (FTA) by the chief executives of the three REC Secretariats; and a Summit of Heads of State and Government of the Tripartite RECs in Kampala, Uganda in 2008 resulted in far-reaching decisions in the areas of trade and customs (FTA); Joint Competition Authority (JCA) for air transport; infrastructure development; legal and institutional framework and; merger of the RECs. Progress is currently being made in the agreed areas (SADC 2011b). The FTA document has been considered for ratification by member states and it is hoped to take off in 2012 (Mwapachu 2010). The fact that the Task Force is managing the process implies that some powers will be delegated to it by the states to make it function. As it performs its functions, more power and authority may eventually be accorded to it on the bases of need and exigencies. The Task Force could ultimately be the umbilical cord that will usher in the fusion of the different regional institutions. Already, the Task Force is establishing relations with outsiders, such as development partners of the RECs. It has signed MOUs with the UK Department for International Development (DFID), for the establishment of the North-South (Trade) Corridor (NSC), and with Development Bank for Southern Africa. The DFID has contributed UK£ 67 million to the NSC project account (COMESA-EAC-SADC Tripartite 2010). An investment committee was established by the MOU to consider and approve financing of proposals of the tripartite projects. In its first sitting, the Committee considered and approved a budget amounting to US$ 10 million for 2010 (Mwapachu 2010). This power of allocation of resources, if it is sustained, will no doubt enhance supra-regional institutions to take up the global administration of harmonized programmes and projects of the RECs.

Inter-regionalism as an approach will no doubt provide a theoretical support for the ECA, AU and the RECs – ECOWAS-UEMAO and COMESA-EAC-SADC Tripartite Task Force – to mobilize resources and support for their actions. It also suggests a procedure for attaining their goal of building stronger, effective and efficient RECs/ building blocks for the African Economic Community (AEC).

Conclusion

'Multiple regionalisms' constitute an obstacle to the integration of Africa. They have caused disruption in Africa's quest for an economic community. The solution to this problem lies in adopting and promoting *inter-regionalism*. As a policy tool, *inter-regionalism* can be used to develop and transform existing mechanisms put in place to address the problem of multiple regionalisms in Africa. Some of these mechanisms are the legal and institutional structures contrived by the AU and some of the RECs to overcome challenges posed by multiple regional groupings. These are, for instance, the Abuja Treaty, the Protocol on Relations between the African Union and the

RECs, and treaties and initiatives in some of the RECs, such as the ECOWAS/ UEMOA Joint Secretariat and the COMESA-EAC-SADC Tripartite Free Trade Area (FTA) project. These structures may provide the foundations for the adoption and implementation of *inter-regionalism*, both as a strategy and a mechanism for effective regional governance and integration of Africa. Our position is that pursuing *inter-regionalism* will help promote the integration of Africa. This is important in view of the fact that the consensus within Africa is that integration is a strategy for pooling resources to overcome the problems of economic *dysfunctionalism*, security challenges and political instability facing the continent.

References

AEC, 2003, 'History and Present Status', Department of Foreign Affairs, OAU Headquarters, Addis Ababa, http://www.dfa.gov.za/foreign/Multilateral/africa/aec.htm, accessed 8 May 2011.

AfDevInfo, 2006, 'Economic Community of Central African States', http://www. afdevinfo.com/htmlreports/org/org_48757.html, accessed 24 January 2010

Aggarwal, V.K. and Fogarty, E.A. 2003, *Explaining Trends in EU Interregionalism*. Available at http://basc.berkeley.edu/pdf/articles/Explaining%20Trends%20in% 20EU%20Interregionalism.pdf

Aggarwal, V.K. and Fogarty, E.A. (eds) 2004, *European Union Trade Strategies: Between Globalism and Regionalism*, Basingstoke: Palgrave, Macmillan).

AMU, 2011, 'History', http://www.maghrebarabe.org/en/uma.cfm, accessed 24 January.

ARIA, 2002, 'Annual Report on Integration in Africa (ARIA-2002)',www.uneca.org, accessed 12 March 2011.

AU, 1991, *Treaty Establishing the African Economic Community*, African Union Commission, Addis Ababa, http://www.africa-union.org/root/au/Documents/Treaties/Text/ AEC_Treaty_1991.pdf, accessed 24 January 2011.

AU, 1998, 'Protocol on Relations between The African Union (AU) and the Regional Economic Communities (RECs)', AU Commission, Addis Ababa, http://www4.worldbank.org/ afr/ssatp/Resources/HTML/legal_review/Annexes/Annexes%20III/Annex%20III-04.pdf, accessed 20 June 2011.

Awoumou, C.D.G., 2008, 'ECCAS or CEMAC Which Regional Economic Community for Central Africa?' Institute for Security Studies, Monograph 155, pp. 109-138 in Ayangafac, C. (ed.) *The Political Economy of Regionalization in Central Africa*, http://www.issafrica.org/ uploads/M155FULL.PDF, accessed 24 January 2011.

BBC, 2008, 'African free trade zone is agreed', British Broadcasting Corporation http:// news.bbc.co.uk/2/hi/business/7684903.stm, accessed 24 January 2011

Bergstein, F., 2010, 'Open Regionalism', Peterson Institute for International Economics, Working Paper 97-3, http://www.iie.com/publications/wp/wp.cfm?ResearchID=152, accessed 20 June 2011.

CEN SAD, 2011, 'Community of Sahel Saharan States' (CEN SAD), Regional Economic Communities (RECs), http://www.africa-union.org/root/au/recs/cen_sad.htm accessed 20 May 2011.

COMESA-EAC-SADC Tripartite, 2010, 'Memorandum of Understanding I Tripartite (COMESA, EAC & SADC) and the Department for International Development (DFID)', COMESA-EAC-SADC Tripartite Greater Regional Harmonization and Cooperation, http://www.comesa-eac-sadc-tripartite.org/node/95, accessed 20 June 2011

Department of Foreign Affairs, Republic of South Africa, 2003, 'African Union in a Nutshell', Department of International Relations and Cooperation, Republic of South Africa

EAC, 2011, 'About EAC' East Africa Community, http://www.eac.int/index.php?option =com_content&view=article&id=1:welcome-to-eac&catid=34:body-text-area&Itemid=53, accessed 24 January 2011.

ECA, 2006, 'Assessing Regional Integration in Africa II: Rationalizing Regional Economic Communities', Economic Commission for Africa and African Union, www.uneca.org, accessed 24 January 2011.

ECOWAS Bulletin, 2011, '7th Meeting of UEMOA/ECOWAS Joint Technical Secretariat: For a better synergy in the conduct of common projects and programs', *The West African Integration Bulletin. http://news.ecowas.int/presseshow.php?nb=260&lang=en&annee=2011,* accessed 20 June 2011.

ECOWAS, 2003, *ECOWAS Revised Treaty*, Abuja, ECOWAS Secretariat.

ECOWAS, 2011, 'Joint ECOWAS-UEMOA Committee Agrees Roadmap for Regional Common External Tariff', ECOWAS Commission, http://news.ecowas.int/presseshow.php?nb=260&lang=en&annee=2011, accessed 20 June 2011.

Gilson, J., 2005, 'New *Interregionalism?* The EU and East Asia', in *European Integration,* Vol.27, No. 3, 307-326, ISSN 0703–6337 Print/ISSN 1477–2280 Online/05/030307-20 © 2005 Taylor and Francis.

GNA, 2004, 'ECOWAS-UEMOA Sign cooperation agreement', www.modernghana.com/newsarchives, accessed 8 May 2010.

Hänggi, H., Roloff, R. and Rüland, J., 2006, '*Interregionalism*: A New Phenomenon in International Relations', in: H Hänggi, R. Roloff & J.Rüland (eds) *Interregionalism and International Relations,* Abingdon: Routledge.

Hänggi, H., 2000, '*Interregionalism*: empirical and theoretical perspectives', Paper prepared for the workshop 'Dollars, Democracy and Trade: External Influence on Economic Integration in the Americas'. The Pacific Council on International Policy, Los Angeles and Council for Applied Policy Research, Munich.

IGAD, 2011, 'IGAD Profile', http://www.africa-union.org/recs/igad_profile.pdf, accessed 8 May 2010.

L'UEMOA, 2003, *Traite Modifié de L'UEMOA,* http://www.uemoa.int/Documents/TraitReviseUEMOA.pdf, accessed 12 March 2011.

Mangeni, F., 2007, 'Economic Partnership Agreement: Background the idea of EPA negotiations', Regional Trade Policy Advisory, www.africa-union.org, accessed 8 May 2010.

Mwapachu, J.V. 2010, 'Report by the Chair of the Tripartite Task Force July, 2010', www.uneca.org, accessed 12 March 2011.

Ncube, M. 2009, 'CEN SAD-The Community of Sahel-Saharan States', United Nations Economic Commission Africa, www.uneca.org, 12 March 2011.

Rüland, J., 2002, '*Interregionalism* in International Relations', Conference Summary, Freiburg, Germany, Arnold-Bergstraesser-Institute.

Rüland, J., 2001, 'ASEAN and the European Union: A Bumpy Interregional Relations', Centre for European Integration Studies, Bonn, Universitat.

SACU, 2011, 'About SACU' Southern African Customs Union, http://www.sacu.int/about.php?id=394, accessed 20 June 2011.

SADC, 2011a, 'About SADC' Southern African Development Community, http://www.sadc.int/english/about-sadc/, accessed 20 June 2011.

SADC, 2011b, 'Communiqué of the Second COMESA-EAC-SADC Tripartite Summit', Southern African Development Community, http://www.sadc.int/english/current-affairs/news/communique-of-the-second-comesa-eac-sadc-tripartite-summit/, accessed 20 June 2011.

Sanankoua, A., 2011, 7th Meeting of UEMOA/ECOWAS Joint Technical Secretariat, Regional Indicative Programme for West Africa (RIP), http://www.pir-rip.ecowas.int/non-class%C3%A9-en/7th-meeting-of-uemoaecowas-joint-technical-secretariat-2/?lang=en, accessed 20 September 2011.

Tadesse, D., 2009, 'The RECs as Building Blocks towards an Effective Continental Integration', Institute for Security Studies (ISS), http://www.issafrica.org/pgcontent.php?UID=28121, accessed 20 June 2011.

2

Regional Development Poles and Self-sustaining Development in Africa

Benaiah Yongo-Bure

Introduction

Diversification and industrialization of African economies are necessary to establish integrated self-sustaining economies in the continent. Even if the service sector has become the largest in most developed economies, the tertiary sector is heavily dependent on the manufacturing sector. Capital goods manufacturing is the most dynamic sub-sector of industry. It has strong backward and forward linkages to the rest of the economy. It supplies inputs to various sub-sectors of industry as well as to agriculture and the service sectors. Given the small sizes of most African countries and the political difficulties of the separate small political entities pursuing a common development policy, African unity and regional integration have been the strategies suggested to achieve self-sustaining development in Africa. But success in regional and eventual continental integration has lagged. Hence, there is the need for additional strategies to initiate self-sustaining development in the continent.

The strategy of Regional Development Poles (RDPs) places emphasis on economic transformation of the few large African countries that can industrialize on their own, given their huge natural and human resources as well as their large domestic markets. From the RDPs, faster economic development will diffuse to the surrounding smaller African countries. The diffusion will be accelerated by establishing inter-African infrastructural networks.

The urge for heavy industrialization, anchored in Africa, arises from the fact that heavy manufacturing industry has profound impact on the rest of the economy through its strong backward and forward linkages. Manufacturing, especially of capital goods, is the most dynamic sub-sector of industry. It is capital-intensive, technologically dynamic and is characterized by economies of scale as many indivisibilities and highly-skilled labour are involved in their construction and operations. The small fragmented markets of most individual African economies cannot support the establishment of capital goods industries. Unless established on a regional basis, such industries would be underutilized in most individual African countries. Effective regional integration would provide African countries with the opportunity to pool their markets and resources. In many cases, technologies designed for developed countries are not suited for African countries at their present stages of development. By establishing capital goods industries in Africa, major technological progress will be internalized in the continent; and in the long-run, such developments will introduce flexibility in the African industry as further technological progress will be internally generated. Consequently, future internally manufactured machinery and equipment designs will keep pace with the required changes in manufacturing consistent with changes in the pattern of demand as development in Africa advances.

Capital goods manufactured in developed countries have become increasingly sophisticated, automated and computerized, and labour-saving. What is still usable in Africa has to be discarded because of lack of spare parts whose production has been discontinued in the developed countries because of technological changes. Most needed consumer durables in Africa such as cars, televisions, videos, and others do not need some of the gadgets installed in them by manufacturers in the developed countries. Yet these expensive products have to be imported as manufactured due to the lack of domestic production in most parts of Africa. These types of products are not consistent with most needs of the African countries except for the demands of the few African elites whose incomes and consumption patterns are similar to those in industrialized countries. Had such goods been produced in Africa, their technological requirements would have progressed along with the changes in the pattern of demand in Africa. They would not be discarded for new ones or the domestic manufacture of the replacements would have generated more jobs in Africa, thus adding to the dynamism necessary for African development.

Industrialization Policy in Africa

Conscious industrialization policies in African countries, like in most underdeveloped countries, began in the post-World War II period. Since most of the developed countries were industrial while the underdeveloped countries were primary producers, economic development came to be identified with industrialization. The prices of industrial exports persistently increased relative to those of primary products. Export prices of primary products were unstable and tended to decline over time. The markets for primary products were stagnant, and primary products were easily substitutable with synthetics. Hence, primary-export-led growth was to be substituted with industrialization (Prebisch 1959; Singer 1950).

Having decided to industrialize, the underdeveloped countries planned to substitute their industrial imports with local production, as their imports were indicative of what could be manufactured domestically. This was the policy of import substitution industrialization. It was thought that underdeveloped economies would progress from the simpler level of manufacturing consumer goods to intermediate goods and to an all-round manufacture of capital goods.

Import substitution was expected to improve the balance of payments as more manufactured imports would be produced domestically. Tariffs were imposed to protect the infant industries from foreign competition. But these tariffs became progressively higher with higher stages of processing. Foreign firms were encouraged to establish tariff factories to overcome the tariff walls. They employed capital-intensive technologies with limited employment opportunities. The capital-intensive industries required more imports of spare parts, raw materials, and replacement capital goods, thus requiring more foreign exchange to operate. Consequently, more resources were being devoted to the urban industries than to the agricultural sector. Rural-urban migration increased, but the capital-intensive industries had limited employment effect. Hence, urban unemployment increased, leading to very serious social and political problems, particularly as most of the unemployed migrants were politically-conscious secondary school leavers.

Because of the limitations of import substitution industrialization, underdeveloped countries changed their industrialization strategy to manufacturing for export. The export of manufactures strategy was recommended particularly for small economies with limited domestic markets (Todaro and Smith 2009). At the early stages of manufacturing, most underdeveloped countries produced similar products, and could not absorb much of each other's products. Tariffs in the developed economies progressively increased with the degree of manufactured imports from the underdeveloped economies. Given the barriers to the export of manufactures, underdeveloped countries embarked on promoting regional integration so as to pool their markets. But while the cooperating and integrating countries could see the joint benefits of integration, they could not easily agree on equitable sharing of these potential benefits. The partner states were at different levels of industrialization, and each partner wanted to accelerate its own rate of industrialization and development. This outlook at integration has not changed much in the continent, hence the slow pace of integration in Africa.

Need for Large Political Units

The quest for collective self-reliance has been advanced by African leaders in various forms since the beginnings of the decolonization movements. There have been calls for African unity, regional cooperation and integration. These calls were premised on the understanding that the many small African countries cannot individually be viable political and economic entities in the international environment of the second half of the twentieth century.[1] Hence, African unity or African integration is a strategy for African development. It is not to follow development but to precede it; or both integration and development should be pursued simultaneously. The argument that each country should solve its problem before integration occurs is spurious because lack of capacity is an integral part of the failure of development. If each small country could achieve its development on its own, there would be no need to integrate. Lack of comprehension of this reality led African countries to fall back from the 1980s to recycling the same colonial economic policies.

The economic problems of the 1970s and 1980s led African countries to revert to the colonial economic policies of market fundamentalism, free trade, and the encouragement of foreign capital. But these were the fundamentals of the colonial economic policies which led Africa to where it was at independence. Hence, there is no wonder that since the institution of the structural adjustment policies in Africa, poverty has become widespread and deepened. The inappropriateness of the colonial-type policies was exhaustively discussed in the 1960s and 1970s, but because African governments desperately wanted foreign aid, they were willing to disregard the arguments against such policies so that they could qualify for foreign aid. The colonial economies were based on the export of primary products to the colonial metropolis. The surplus from the export earnings was not reinvested in the colonial economies, but channelled to the colonial powers. This pattern of trade still persists in most African countries. Sustainable industrialization of tiny economies is hardly possible, particularly in a world of long-established competitors in the world market. Hence, it was inevitable that the industrialization policies of the early post-independence era were not sustainable for most African countries.

The African colonial economies boomed with the production of export crops and minerals but left Africa unindustrialized. The performance of the export crops and hence of the African economies fluctuated with the business cycle in Europe, which was the dominant market for African exports. Most African economies have shown impressive growth records during the first decade of the twenty-first century as Africa has diversified its export markets. With increasing Asian, particularly Chinese and Indian, demand for African minerals, many African countries have been able to substantially withstand the negative repercussions of the Great Recession of 2007-2010. Africa should take advantage of the current surge in Asian demand for the continent's raw materials to establish major capital goods industries in the continent. This will lead to self-sustaining development in the continent even after the demand for African raw materials subsides.

The increasing deterioration in the African economies, from the 1970s and the impact of the structural adjustment policies of the 1980s, led African countries to intensify their efforts towards regional integration. This led to the adoption of the Lagos Plan of Action by the African Heads of State and Government in 1980. This act culminated in the signing of the Abuja Treaty of 1991, promulgating the African Economic Community (AEC), which came into force in 1994.[2]

The establishment of the AEC was to be phased in six stages. Stage one was to involve the creation of regional blocs or Regional Economic Communities (RECs) where such do not yet exist. This process was to be completed by 1999. The RECs were to be the building blocks of the African Economic Community (AEC). The second stage was the strengthening of intra-REC integration and inter-REC harmonization, which was to be completed in 2007. Stage three was to consist of the establishment of a free trade area and customs union in each regional bloc by the end of 2017. The establishment of an Africa-wide customs union was the fourth stage and was to be achieved by the end of 2019. The fifth stage was to be the establishment of a continent-wide common market, the African Common Market (ACM) by 2023. The sixth stage was to be the establishment of a continent-wide economic and monetary union by the end of 2028. The transitional period, during which all these structures were to be set up, would end by 2034 at the latest (UNECA 2008).

The Common Market of Eastern and Southern Africa (COMESA), the East African Community (EAC), the Economic Community of Central African States (ECCAS), the Economic Community of West African States (ECOWAS), the Southern Africa Development Community (SADC), among others, are clear manifestations of the African leaders' recognition of the need for larger units in Africa to achieve viable development in the current world environment. However, to date, only the East African Community has progressed to having a common market, and few have attained even the effective stage of free trade areas. Hence, as much as African leaders seem to appreciate the importance of collective African self-reliance, their political rhetoric on African integration has so far not been accompanied by commensurate actions. Consequently, multiple regional groupings have been established in the continent, many of which have overlapping memberships. Trade between the member states is riddled with many restrictions, especially by non-trade barriers. Hence, the results of regional integration in Africa have been modest.

The member countries of the regional groupings have similar production structures. Most of them lack a strong industrial base to produce diversified manufactured products for trade within the groupings. Their multiple currencies are not convertible. The cost of doing intra- and inter- regional blocs business is high due to a host of non-tariff barriers such as poor infrastructure, duplicative border procedures and cumbersome paper requirements. The free movements of people and the right of establishment have progressed in some groupings, but not in many African sub-regions. Non-tariff barriers such as customs officials, police roadblocks, and constant harassment by immigration officials hamper free trade. Hence, the attainment of the goals of regional integration will take time. The processes of realizing the RECs and the AEC will be slow and long. In the meanwhile, major technological changes will not wait for Africa to integrate. Such a situation will perpetuate Africa's follower-status in the challenges of globalization.

To influence the direction of globalization and hence, the continent's destiny, Africa must internalize the processes of technological progress within a short period. The challenge of fast internalizing substantial technological changes within Africa should be focused on the large African countries that should muster the political leadership to turn their potentials into regional development poles in the continent. Development in the continental regional development poles will diffuse faster to the rest of the African countries given their proximities within the continent.

Regional Development Poles

The colonial economies of Africa were founded when the continent was parcelled into European estates. Unfortunately, after about 50 years of formal independence, the African elites have not transformed the inherited deformed economies. These economies have either persisted or collapsed, instead of being transformed. Most African economies can hardly be transformed within the existing domestic structures, although a few large ones can. The Democratic Republic of Congo (DR Congo), Ethiopia, Nigeria, and South Africa are among the few African countries with the human and natural resource capable of being transformed into self-sustaining economies (UNECA 2012).[3] South Africa is already a self-sustaining industrial economy, and exports industrial products to virtually all African countries. If more large African countries industrialize, the integration of African economies within Africa will be enhanced and therefore lead to less dependence on external global factors. In this way African countries will have larger capacity to withstand external global shocks.

The African Union, the New Partnership for African Development (NEPAD), the Economic Commission for Africa, the African Development Bank, among others, and the elites of the respective countries, should lead in the establishment of viable development poles in the continent. Given that each country is different, with different endowment and initial conditions, the elites of each country are in a better position to identify the relevant policies for their country's achievement of economic transformation and self-sustaining development. But regular joint brain-storming with other experts in these countries would allow for the exchange of relevant experiences and perspectives. Self-sustaining development to the rest of the countries in the continent will diffuse from the regional development poles faster than from outside the continent.

The establishment of diversified industrial economies, financial systems, and convertible currencies in the regional development poles will help strengthen the small neighbouring economies. For example, the small economies in southern Africa have benefited greatly from the de facto Common Currency Area (CCA) in the region anchored on the convertible South African Rand. This is because of the strong South African economy. Even if these southern African countries lacked foreign exchange, they would easily acquire the Rand and procure their industrial import requirements from South Africa. Moreover, migration for employment within the continent will be easier, cheaper and less risky.[4]

The creation of development poles in Africa is to be based on the large physical sizes, resource bases and populations of the large countries. But this does not mean that the strategy of regional integration should be abandoned. The two strategies should be pursued simultaneously.

To complement the regional development pole and regional integration strategies is the development of regional and trans-Africa infrastructure. For sustainable development to spread throughout the continent, the various parts of the continent have to be linked with elaborate and efficient infrastructure. Africa's infrastructural deficit is put at $93 billion annually until 2020 (AfDB Sept. 2010). Trans-African and regional highways, railways and electricity grids have been mapped since the 1970s and 1980s (UNECA 1986). It is time for serious implementation. Great hydroelectric potentials such as the Inga Falls in the Congo DR could be developed to supply large parts of the continent. Africa can also tap its solar and wind energy resources.

Currently, less than 40 per cent of the continent's population has access to electricity; about a third of the rural population has access to roads; and only 5 per cent of agriculture is under irrigation. Only about 34 per cent of the population has access to improved sanitation and about 65 per cent to clean water (AfDB Sept. 2010).

The Information and Communications Technology (ICT) sub-sector is characterized by huge differences across specific services. Access to mobile phones averaged four out of ten in 2008, with penetration rates growing fastest in the world. However, internet access averaged 80 persons per 1,000. Fixed telephone figures are the lowest, reflecting the limited access to electricity.

In addition, Africa faces higher access costs relative to other underdeveloped countries. Africa's freight is about four times more expensive, power costs 14 cents per kilowatt hour against 5-10 cents; and mobile telephony costs $12 per month compared with $8 elsewhere (AfDB Sept. 2010).

The statistics on Africa's transportation system are poor and need to be urgently addressed, otherwise the quest for accelerated development in Africa is just a dream. The total road network in sub-Saharan Africa is put at only 204 km per 1,000 km^2 of land area of which only about 25 per cent is paved, compared with the world average of 944 km per 1,000 km^2 of land area. But there are huge intra-African disparities.

Rail transport is more efficient and costs less than road transport for bulky primary commodities such as the majority of Africa's exports. Yet, rail networks are the least developed in the continent. The colonial links of economic enclaves to the ocean ports are still the only major links. Fourteen sub-Saharan African countries have no operational rail networks, while spatial density of operational rail ranges from 30 to 50 per million people with a few countries having network densities of more than 400.[5]

Africa also needs to improve its ports. Port capacities need to be expanded and the performance of existing facilities as well as handling costs improved. Connectivity to ports is poor. There is the need for pipelines to link African oil producers with importing countries in the continent. With expansion and improvement in regional and trans-African infrastructure, development in the regional poles will diffuse more easily to all countries in the continent.

Some Examples of Regional Development Poles

Nigeria has all it takes resource-wise to become one of the major world economies; but so far the leadership has failed to utilize that potential effectively. With its abundant natural resources, domestic market of over 160 million people, thousands of highly educated people in various fields, and oil export earnings of over $110 million per day, Nigeria could build a strong diversified economy in the western part of the continent with a profound impact on western and equatorial Africa, and even beyond. Moreover, as the Gulf of Guinea becomes major oil producer and exporter, Nigeria could coordinate the development of a large petroleum-products manufacturing industries in the region, including the islands (Ghazvinian 2007).

African oil exporting countries have to channel their petro-funds into restructuring their economies. However, with tiny domestic markets and other resources, most of them cannot transform their economies individually. Instead of corrupt elites squandering these resources abroad, some regional hegemonies should coordinate their use for the transformation of the regional economy.

Before the oil industry came to dominate the Nigerian economy, the country produced its own food supplies and exported large quantities of cocoa, cotton, cattle, hides and skins, groundnuts, palm oil and palm kernels. Renewed emphasis on the agricultural sector would expand the domestic market and further enhance the country's efforts in building a huge self-sustaining industrial economy.

DR Congo, located in the centre of Africa, probably has the greatest potential for building a viable economy if it can realize its potential. It could learn from Brazil as there is hardly much difference between the Congo and Brazil in terms of natural resource endowment. Congo has agricultural, mineral, forestry, fisheries, hydroelectric potentials, population and central location.

The exploitation of the Inga hydro-electric potential alone can earn the Congo billions of dollars from exports to others parts of Africa, while enhancing power supply in many parts of the continent. The foreign exchange can be used to develop a diversified economy (Fall 2010; World Bank 2009). Meanwhile, Congo's mineral and other natural resources can generate tremendous earnings for the country's own national, provincial and local development. The combination of DR Congo's tremendous energy and mineral potentials could produce a major industrial giant on the world level. Metallurgical and chemical industries could be developed from local resources. These industries would make it possible to establish large machine tools and engineering industries. A range of spare parts could be produced from the large machine tools industry (Alemayehu 2000). Given DR Congo's central location in the continent, its access to various countries for market would be cost effective, especially with the establishment of regional and trans-African infrastructure.

Moreover, given its huge forest and the environmental impact of poverty in the country, the development and electrification of DR Congo would deter major region-wide climatic changes. Raising the living standards of the Congolese considerably will lessen dependence on the natural environment for food, fuel and building materials; and hence avert catastrophic climatic changes resulting from environmental degradation. The damaging impact of the Cold War on the Congo has delayed but not destroyed the country's potential to become one of the world's major economies. Developing this potential will have wide positive consequences in Africa.

South Africa has already established a strong manufacturing economy. South Africa is the world's largest producer of chrome, manganese, platinum, vanadium, and vermiculite; the second largest producer of gold and other minerals. It is also the world's third largest exporter of coal. Its mineral wealth, and its strong manufacturing and financial sectors, have made South Africa the strongest economy in the continent. It is already having an important impact on development in Africa, especially in southern, eastern and central Africa. South Africa is also a net exporter of farm products.

However, the continuation of the apartheid era pattern of land ownership needs a major reform so that many South Africans can benefit from the prosperity of the country. The reforms instituted so far have made insignificant impact on the lives of the landless and the many unemployed. Without addressing the land issue and the problems of unemployment and inequalities, the South African society faces the risk of polarizing the races which could lead to social upheavals. For a viable and sustainable development to prevail, the bulk of the population must benefit from it.

A dynamic industrial South Africa has reduced dependence of many countries in the sub-region on long-distance imports of development inputs, and this has helped accelerate development in the region. South African manufactured goods and telecommunications products are exported to many other African countries. In 2011, South Africa joined the BRICS, a club of emerging industrial economies consisting of Brazil (B), Russia (R), India (I), China (C), and South Africa (S). South Africa is addressing its problem of shortages of energy by importing electricity from DR Congo.

Although Ethiopia has a huge area of arid land, it has many large rivers such as the Blue Nile (Abay), Awash, Barro, Omo and Wabe Shebelle. It can irrigate large areas and generate large amounts of hydro-electric power, some of which can be exported. Moreover, its mineral potential has not yet been tapped. Its recent policy step of expanding graduate programmes in its universities greatly will soon enhance the capabilities of its human resources tremendously. With its fast-growing population and large arid lands, industrialization becomes imperative as an industrial economy has greater capacity to sustain a large population.

In addition to focusing on the development of its human resources, Ethiopia is also targeting its huge hydro-electric potential of 45,000 megawatts that ranks it the second to DR Congo in Africa. The country has for a decade now been implementing an ambitious programme of hydro-electric development. It plans to increase electricity access to about 75 per cent of its population by July 2015 (Block and Strzepek 2012). Ethiopia's largest hydro electric dams include Fincha (1973), Gilgel Gibe (2004), Tekeze (2009), Beles (2010), Gilgel Gibe II (2011) and Gilgel Gibe III (2013). The latest and largest dam planned is the Millennium Dam on the Blue Nile, near the Sudan border. More dams are planned.[6]

Since May 2011, Ethiopia has been exporting electricity to Djibouti. A transmission line to export power to Sudan is under construction. Ethiopia also plans to export power to Kenya. The Ethiopian-Kenyan transmission line will be linked through Tanzania to southern Africa through a power pool project for eastern and southern Africa.

Ethiopia's power development programme is not limited to hydro electricity. It is also developing its potential in solar, wind and geothermal energy. It is even experimenting with energy production from crops such as castor seeds and jatropha (Bayissa 2008). Ethiopia, Kenya and South Sudan are to develop a large seaport at Lamu on the Kenyan coast. Ethiopia will be linked to the Lamu port by road and railway. By all indications, Ethiopia is embarking on a major economic transformation using its comparative advantage in energy resources. It seems to be succeeding, as its gross domestic product grew at an annual average rate of eight to ten per cent during the first decade of the twenty-first century (IMF 2011).

Concluding Remarks

Diversification and industrialization of the African economies are essential for integrated, self-sustaining economic development in Africa. Industrialization in the continent, with the manufacture of capital goods occupying a significant place, will lead to internalization of significant technological progress since technology is embodied in capital goods. Major technological developments within the continent will lead to self-sustaining economic growth and the development in the regional development poles with considerable spread effects in the region. Hence, industrialization of the African economies must be accorded high priority.

Many African leaders had the correct instincts at independence but could not sustain the focus. As economic problems mounted, they shifted to attending to immediate short-term crises, especially from the 1980s. However, given the small sizes of most African countries, each one of them cannot individually establish a dynamic capital goods manufacturing sub-sector. Consequently, most of the manufacturing in all African countries consists of consumer goods industries and the processing of primary products.

Aware of the limitations of their countries' abilities to industrialize individually, African leaders advocated African unity, or at least regional integration, as the appropriate solutions to overcoming the problem of size. So far, however, their legal and political conceptions of sovereignty have superseded their vision of economic necessity for larger political units. If African leaders persist with their view of narrow sovereignty, the continent will continue to be subservient in the increasingly globalizing international economy as the goal of regional and eventual continental integration will be hard to achieve. Consequently, the establishment of viable self-sustaining economies in Africa will be a distant dream.

While African countries should continue with the efforts at collective action, those large enough to go it on their own should spearhead the processes of diversification and industrialization through their own national efforts so as to speed up industrial and technological development in the continent. The diffusion of industrialization from these African regional development poles to the rest of Africa will be faster than from outside the continent as it happens in contagious economies in other parts of the world. Not all African countries are disadvantaged due to balkanization. But for the regional development poles to have major region-wide effects, the scale of development must be substantial. The regional impacts of the development of small economies that have attained middle-income status have been negligible. Even the impact of prosperity within the small African middle-income countries is limited to the elites and few areas of the countries where mining and/or manufacturing take place. There is not much distinction in the living conditions of the rural and informal urban sector in the small middle-income and the low-income countries. For development to be meaningful to the country and the region, its benefits should spread to the bulk of the population. This is only possible through a dynamic integrated industrial economy with the production of capital goods featuring prominently in the industrial structure.

Notes

1. The nineteenth-century conditions that enabled small European countries to develop do not exist today. Consequently, small African countries cannot hope to develop as small European countries once did. Although small countries can industrialize, they cannot drive their own destiny for very long. The twenty-first century is being billed as the 'Chinese Century' just as the twentieth century was labelled the 'American Century'. Hong Kong, Japan, Singapore, South Korea and Taiwan could not claim the twentieth century, even though their economies underwent major transformations, because none of these economies were as dominant as that of the United States.

   China's transformation is being determined by the Chinese themselves, enabled by the country's huge resources and large domestic market. Instead of telling China what to do, large foreign companies do what China asks them to do. Hence, they readily make their technology available to China, overlook China's piracy of their patents, and willingly undertake research and development in China.

2. The Treaty of June 1991 established the African Economic Community (AEC). This was a realization of the Lagos Plan of Action of 1980 adopted by the then Organization of African Unity (OAU), now the African Union (AU).

3. As at mid-2011, thirteen sub-Saharan African countries had populations of about 20 million and above as follows (in millions): Nigeria (162.5), Ethiopia (84.7), DR Congo (67.8), South Africa (50.5), Tanzania (46.2), Kenya (41.6), Uganda (34.5), Ghana (25.0), Mozambique (23.9), Madagascar (21.3), Cote d'Ivoire (20.2), Cameroon (20.0), and Angola (19.6).

4. Many African migrants have perished while crossing the Sahara Desert and the Mediterranean Sea for jobs in Europe.

5. Europe's densities range from 200 to 1,000.

6. The figures in brackets are the dates of completion of the projects. Also see *http://www.ethio-energy-development.blogspot.com*

References

African Development Bank, AfDB, 2010, *Economic Brief, Vol. 1*, September Issue, Tunis.

African Development Bank, AfDB, 2010, *African Economic Conference: Agenda for Africa's Economic Recovery and Long Term Growth,* Tunis.

Alemayehu, Makonnen, 2000, *Industrializing Africa: Development Options and Challenges for the 21st Century,* Trenton, NJ & Asmara, Africa World Press.

Bayissa, Bekele, 2008, 'A Review of the Ethiopian Energy Policy and Biofuels Strategy', in Yaye Assefa, ed., *Digest of Ethiopia's National Policies, Strategies, and Programs,* Addis Ababa, Forum for Social Studies, pp. 209-238.

Block, Paul and Kenneth Strzepek, 2012, 'Power Ahead: Meeting Ethiopia's Energy Needs Under a Changing Climate', *Review of Development Economics,* 16(3), pp. 476-488.

Carbaugh, Robert J., 2009, *International Economics,* Mason, Ohio, South-Western Cengage Learning.

Fall, Latsoucabe, 2010, 'Harnessing the Hydropower Potential in Africa: What should be the Place and Role of Grand Inga Hydropower Project', XX1st World Energy Congress, Montreal, Canada, 12-16 September.

Ghazvinian, John, 2007, *Untapped: The Scramble for Africa's Oil,* New York, Harcourt, Inc.

International Monetary Fund (IMF), 2011, *Regional Economic Outlook: Sub-Saharan Africa: Recovery and New Risks,* Washington, D C, April.

Metzger, Martina, 2008, *Regional Cooperation and Integration in Sub-Saharan Africa, Discussion Papers No. 189,* Geneva, United Nations Conference on Trade and Development.

Prebisch, Raul, 1959, 'Commercial Policy in the Underdeveloped Countries', *American Economic Review* 49 (May), pp. 251-73.

Singer, H. W., 1950, 'The Distribution of Gains between Investing and Borrowing Countries', *American Economic Review* 40 (May), pp. 473-94.

Todaro, Michael P. and Stephen, C. Smith, 2009, *Economic Development.* New York: Pearson Addison Wesley.

United Nations Economic Commission for Africa (UNECA), 1986, *First Combined Meeting of Trans-African Highway Authorities Final Report,* Addis Ababa.

United Nations Economic Commission for Africa (UNECA), 2004, *Assessing Regional Integration in Africa: Policy Research Report,* Addis Ababa.

United Nations Economic Commission for Africa (UNECA), 2006, *Assessing Regional Integration in Africa II: Rationalizing Regional Economic Communities,* Addis Ababa.

United Nations Economic Commission for Africa (UNECA), 2007, *Economic Report on Africa 2007: Accelerating Africa's Development through Diversification,* Addis Ababa.

United Nations Economic Commission for Africa (UNECA), 2008, *Assessing Regional Integration in Africa III: Towards Monetary and Financial Integration in Africa,* Addis Ababa.

United Nations Economic Commission for Africa (UNECA), 2010, *Assessing Regional Integration in Africa IV: Enhancing Intra-African Trade,* Addis Ababa.

United Nations Economic Commission for Africa (UNECA), 2011, *Economic Report on Africa 2011: Governing Development in Africa- the role of the state in economic transformation,* Addis Ababa.

United Nations Economic Commission for Africa (UNECA), 2012, *African Statistical Yearbook 2012,* Addis Ababa.

World Bank, 2005, *African Development Indicators*, Washington, D C.

World Bank, 2005, *World Development Indicators*, Washington, D C.

World Bank, 2009, 'DR Congo Power Plant Holds Promise for Energy Supply to Millions in Africa', Washington, DC.

World Bank, 2012, 'World Bank Approves New Power Transmission Line between Ethiopia and Kenya to Boost Electricity and Economic Growth in East Africa', Washington, D C.

3

Interrogating Regional Security Arrangements in Africa: The Case of the African Peace and Security Architecture

Leah Kimathi

The concept of a peace and security architecture refers to structures, norms, capacities and procedures that are employed to avert conflict and war, to mediate for peace where a conflict has broken out as well as to ensure the general maintenance of peace and security in a given setting. These instruments and norms may be well set up by way of a blueprint, with clearly defined inter-relationships, or they may be in the process of growth and definition where there is a framework of the architecture that is continually evolving and adjusting to changing circumstances. As a continental master plan for peace and security, the African Peace and Security Architecture (APSA) falls more in the latter than in the former category. While the general layout is in place, its implementation is still in the process of growth and refinement so that it can ultimately and holistically respond to the peace and security requirements of the African continent.

APSA has its origins in the formative years of the now defunct Organization of African Unity (OAU). The OAU divided the continent into five regions, aligned with a number of existing Regional Economic Communities (RECs) and prompting the establishment of others. While Africa's regional organizations were originally designed as centre points for regional economic development, regional bodies and leaders quickly acknowledged that the insecurity and instability endemic in the regions were major impediments to integration and development (Mwanasali 2003; Olonisakin and Ero 2003). With the exception of the Arab Magreb Union, all of Africa's RECs have subsequently developed security mechanisms with varying competencies to operate within the context of a broader regional integration agenda (Powell 2005).

The OAU became engaged in conflict resolution in Africa almost from its inception in 1963, but restricted its efforts to settling border disputes and adjudicating ideological differences resulting from the Cold War (Amoo 1993). The OAU Charter recognized the peaceful settlement of disputes through mediation, conciliation and arbitration. A Commission for Mediation, Conciliation and Arbitration was established, but the protocol prescribing optional jurisdiction and mediation was limited to inter-state disputes. These restrictions eventually made the commission redundant (Francis 2007). In response to the security challenges and threat perceptions of the 1960s, the OAU proposed the establishment of an African High Command as a collective security and defence framework. The aims of the high command were: to ensure protection of territorial integrity; to help guard political sovereignty; to set up a defence against external aggression; to prevent the balkanization of Africa; and, to assist liberation fighters against colonial domination. Proposals for the creation of sub-regional defence and security mechanisms were made in 1972. Although nothing concrete came from these proposals, they became the blueprints for the formation of sub-regional security and peacekeeping mechanisms. In this way the OAU laid the foundation for a new regional architecture for peace and security (Francis 2007).

With the end of the Cold War, and the inevitable reduction of Africa's strategic importance on the world stage coupled with the crises of the 1990s, the OAU felt the need to change its conflict resolution approach in the continent. This led to the establishment of the Mechanism for Conflict Prevention, Management and Resolution in Cairo in 1993 with the following functions:

- To anticipate and prevent situations of potential conflict from developing into full-blown wars.
- To undertake peace-making and peace-building efforts if full-blown conflicts should arise.
- To carry out peacemaking and peace-building activities in post-conflict situations (Powell 2005).

While the mechanism comprehensively addressed the entire spectrum of conflicts, nothing much by way of implementation was achieved and it therefore met the same fate that had befallen the earlier instruments.

Generally, the OAU was criticized for being ineffective in establishing peace and security within Africa. Perhaps the only mechanism that was relatively successful was the Commission for Mediation, Conciliation and Arbitration in its dealings with issues of decolonization and the eradication of racist regimes (Francis 2007). This commission played a role in ending apartheid in South Africa and decolonization in Namibia and Zimbabwe, but could not end colonial domination in both western Sahara and Eritrea. The major obstacles contributing to the dismal performance of the OAU in the field of peace and security had less to do with the lack of institutional frameworks and mechanisms but more to do with its commitment to the principles of sovereignty and non-interference, as well as respect for established borders and territorial integrity. The cause of the organization's failure to act effectively in this area (i.e., peace and security) was that, with few exceptions, the organization was not legally or operationally equipped to intervene in either inter- or intra-state conflicts.

As a response to the ineffectiveness of the organization's mechanisms, the African leaders decided in May 2001 to devise a new security regime to operate within the framework of the nascent African Union (AU) (Kioko 2003). This transformation ushered in substantive normative and institutional changes representing a move away from strict adherence to non-interference by giving the AU the right to intervene. Human rights and democracy were also given prominence in the AU Constitutive Act and were repeated without fail in almost all of the major instruments subsequently adopted. Among other fundamental principles, the Constitutive Act of the AU gives primacy to the intention to develop closer collaboration with the many and diverse sub-regional economic communities and security defence systems in the pursuit of continental development, peace and security objectives (Francis 2007).

At the institutional level, this transformation most notably saw the emergence of the current African Peace and Security Architecture (Dersso 2010). The architecture is premised on several norms which emanate both from the OAU Charter as well as the AU Constitutive Act. These norms include the sovereign equality of member states (Article 4a); non-intervention by member states (Article 4g); devising African solutions for African problems, non-use of force in the peaceful settlement of disputes (Articles 4e, 4f, 4i); condemnation of unconstitutional changes of government (Article 4p); as well as the right of the AU to intervene in the affairs of a member state in grave circumstances (Article 4h) (Aning 2008).

Components of APSA

APSA is anchored within the AU Peace and Security Council (PSC). The protocol establishing the PSC came into effect in January 2004. According to Article 2 of the PSC protocol, the PSC is central to APSA and is 'a standing decision-making organ for the prevention, management and resolution of conflicts' which operates as 'a collective security and early warning arrangement to facilitate timely and efficient response to conflict and crisis situations in Africa'. Article 2 lists the components of APSA as: i) the AU Commission, ii) a Panel of the Wise, iii) a Continental Early Warning System (CEWS), iv) an African Standby Force (ASF) and v) a Special Fund. These different components of APSA come into play sequentially in the process of the prevention, management and resolution of conflicts.

i) **The AU Commission** is the Secretariat of the Union entrusted with the executive functions. It has several portfolios including the Peace and Security Department (PSD). Within this department are core divisions, Conflict Management, Peace and Support Operations, Defence and Security as well as the Secretariat to the Peace and Security Council. As the central organ of the AU, the Commission plays the important role of being the driving force behind the Union's activities including those of peace and security. It implements, coordinates and documents PSC decisions; it also facilitates networking and linkages between the PSD and other relevant departments and programmes. The Commission also helps member states to implement various programmes and policies and it takes on the strategic role of mobilizing resources for AU financing, including for peace and security. However, the Commission faces various challenges, one of them being inadequate staffing which impacts negatively on inter-departmental coordination and collaboration. This hampers the overall effectiveness of the Commission and that of the PSD (Peace and Security Department 2010).

ii) Article 11 of the PSC protocol establishes the Panel of the Wise in order to support the efforts of the Council and those of the Chairperson of the Commission, particularly in conflict prevention. The Panel is composed of five highly respected African personalities on the basis of regional representation. They are appointed to serve for a three-year term, renewable once, with the following mandate:

- The Panel shall advise the Council and the Chairperson of the Commission on all issues pertaining to the promotion and maintenance of peace, security and stability in Africa.
- The Panel shall undertake all such actions deemed appropriate to support efforts of the Council and those of the Chairperson of the Commission for the prevention of conflicts.
- As and when necessary, the Panel may pronounce itself on any issue relating to the promotion and maintenance of peace, security and stability in Africa, in the form it considers most appropriate (AU 2007).

The current Panel members, appointed in 2007, include:

- Brigalia Bam, Chairperson of the Independent Electoral Commission of South Africa (Southern Africa Region)
- Ahmed Ben Bella, former President of Algeria (North Africa Region)
- Elizabeth Pognon, former President of the Constitutional Court of Benin (West Africa Region)
- Miguel Trovoada, Former Prime Minister and President of Sao Tome and Principe (Central Africa Region)
- Salim Ahmed Salim, former Secretary General of the OAU (East Africa Region).

The Panel, an idea borrowed from African traditions defining the role and place of elders in peacebuilding, is one of the most innovative structures of APSA. As a non-threatening instrument, it can be used to handle issues that are too politically sensitive to be undertaken by the other components of APSA.

However, the Panel is one of the least developed instruments. It was among the last to be operationalized and was officially inaugurated in December 2007 (Heinlein 2007). Its role as a preventive strategy needs to be further elaborated, especially in terms of engagement. Further, the Panel should be included in the AU Commission's structure so as to give it greater visibility and, most crucially, to ensure that it is supported from the AU regular budget. The current reliance on partner support does not bode well for the sustainability and ownership of this instrument (Peace and Security Department 2010).

iii) Article 12 of the PSC Protocol gives rise to the Continental Early Warning System (CEWS). The early warning system is intended to 'facilitate the anticipation and prevention of conflicts'. When fully operational, the system is expected to connect the AU headquarters and the headquarters of regional organizations through a feedback process of relaying information and interventions. The observation and monitoring centre, the 'Situation Room', located in Addis Ababa, is expected to be in continuous communication with other early warning centres within the regional organizations. Having begun in 2006 with the adoption of the *Framework for the Operationalization of the CEWS*, important achievements have been registered especially in setting up and equipping the Situation Room, developing data collection and analysis tools, as well as in the continuous news monitoring and summarization of the *Africa News Brief* and *Daily News Highlights* that are circulated by the AU Commission to a wide network of subscribers, including RECs by email (Kimathi 2010).

In order to fully operationalize CEWS, however, the system faces a number of challenges, mostly emanating from capacity constraints facing both the AU and RECs. With the possible exception of the Economic Community of West African States Early Warning and Response Network (ECOWARN) and the Conflict Early Warning and Response Network (CEWARN) in the Inter-governmental Authority on Development (IGAD), the development of CEWS' basic operational capability in most of the other regional organizations, especially in Southern African Development Community (SADC), East African Community (EAC) and the Common Market for Eastern and Southern Africa (COMESA) is still in its infancy. This is as a result of inadequate staffing, lack of adequate attention given to its development and overreliance on external support, among other challenges. Another critical obstacle facing CEWS throughout the continent is the lack of effective collaboration between AU and other actors such as the civil society and the UN, despite the importance given to these collaborative linkages by the CEWS Framework (Kimathi 2010). There also exist weak linkages between regional CEWS and the Situation Room in Addis Ababa.

iv) The **ASF** represents the peacekeeping capacity of the AU. Its formation was endorsed by the African Heads of State at their summit in Maputo in 2003 (Daley 2006). Given that mobilizing troops for peace operations takes time, the ASF was envisioned to serve in a continental rapid-response capacity for peace support operations and interventions. It has the technical support and backing of a Military Staff Committee (MSC) whose role is to provide technical suggestions and solutions to military issues and to provide their expert opinion to the PSC before military decisions are made (Aning 2008).

According to Article 13 of the PSC protocol, the ASF is to be prepared for rapid deployment in a range of peacekeeping operations, including the following:

- Observation and monitoring missions;
- Other types of peace support missions;

- Intervention in a member state in respect of grave circumstances or at the request of a member state in order to restore peace and security in accordance with Articles 4(h) and (j) of the Constitutive Act;
- Preventive deployment in order to prevent (i) a dispute or a conflict from escalating, (ii) an ongoing conflict from spreading to neighbouring areas or states, and (iii) the resurgence of violence after parties to a conflict have reached an agreement;
- Peace-building, including post-conflict disarmament and demobilization;
- Humanitarian assistance to alleviate the suffering of the civilian population in conflict areas and support efforts to address major natural disasters ; and
- Any other function as may be mandated by the Peace and Security Council or the Assembly (AU 2002).

An integrated force made up of military, civilian and police components, the ASF consists of five regional standby capabilities representing North, East, West, South and Central Africa. Given its mandate, the ASF is one of the most critical elements of the architecture that will enable the AU to deliver on its promise of intervention to protect people who are victims of civil unrest and conflict and to provide prompt and robust response to manage and resolve African crises. It enables the PSC first, to prevent and manage conflicts by containing their spread or escalation; second, to support its peace processes as a peace support mission; and third, to enforce its decisions in cases of grave circumstances or to intervene when necessary (Dersso 2010).

Generally, the five regional components of the ASF had attained an initial operating capability in accordance with the ASF roadmap by 2010 (PSD 2010). Most regions have conducted Level I (Map Exercise), Level II (Command Post Exercise) and also participated in Levels I and II Decision-making Exercises at the continental level (AU Peace Support Operations Division 2010).

Despite the successes, however, ASF is faced with several challenges in its operationalization. The mandate of ASF needs to be further clarified and fine-tuned with regard to the different deployment scenarios, including the role of troop-contributing countries, regional organizations and the AU Commission itself to avoid overlaps and gaps. Legally binding agreements should be negotiated among RECs/ AU and member states regarding troop contribution, since to date, no such agreement exists. The level of coordination and harmonization between the regional planning elements and the AU Peace Support Operations Division (PSOD) needs to be improved for the benefit of the overall effectiveness of the force. This should go hand-in-hand with improving the level of commitment, professionalism and leadership within the AU Commission. While the role of development partners remains central to the success of the ASF, its agenda, whether in training or overall development, should be driven by Africans in response to the continent's peace and security needs. However, this is not always the case and, in some instances, decisions may be taken more to satisfy donor requirements than to answer to the needs of ASF or its components. Ultimately, troop deployment and associated logistics are very expensive exercises and sustainable ways will have to be sought for the purpose of supporting these actions so as to mitigate the challenges associated with overreliance on partners (Dersso 2010; Peace and Security Department 2010; Klingebiel *et al.* 2008).

v) According to Article 21, the Peace Fund was meant to provide the necessary financial resources for peace support missions and other operational activities related to peace and security. It is one of the AU organs inherited from the former OAU. Initially, the Fund was established in 1993 to support the work of the OAU Mechanism for Conflict Prevention, Management and Resolution (AU 2003). In theory, the Peace Fund is supposed to receive six per cent of the operative funds and voluntary contributions from donors and member states (Klingebiel et al 2008). However, this has not been the case. Like the operative fund, voluntary funds are almost entirely provided by donors especially for those earmarked for missions, but these funds do not flow through the Peace Fund, thereby destabilizing it as a key component of APSA. A further drawback is that there are no modalities in place on the use of the fund as well as no strong resource mobilization strategies and mechanisms (Peace and Security Council 2010).

Role of Partners

Sub-regional Organizations and APSA

Sub-regional organizations are considered to be the essential building blocks and implementation agencies of the African Union's many programmes, including APSA. This cooperation ensures that the AU not only profits from the regions' comparative advantage in military and security matters, but also from their experience with peace operations in the case of western, eastern and southern Africa. Further, their established frameworks and mechanisms for conflict prevention, management and resolution grant them a significant stake and a central role in the AU peace and security processes. Under this approach, the primary responsibility for peace and security remains squarely with the regional economic communities, while the AU serves as an authoritative clearinghouse and framework for all initiatives (Oloo 2008). Therefore, sub-regional organizations are expected to set up APSA structures at their levels which work in sync with equivalent structures at the AU level.

To solidify this relationship between the AU and sub-regional organizations and mechanisms, a Memorandum of Understanding defines relations between the two levels in peace and security. The major objectives of this agreement include:

- Contributing to the full operationalization of the Africa Peace and Security Architecture (APSA);
- Ensuring regular information exchange on the activities of the parties to the agreement, and designing ways by which peace/security-related activities can be implemented jointly, in keeping with the principles of the PSC protocol;
- Engaging in a regular review of the contribution of each Regional Economic Community and regional mechanism in the areas of the major components (as discussed earlier in this chapter) of APSA (AU 2007).

In general, therefore, the development and implementation of APSA depends upon the regional organizations, without whose cooperation and commitment APSA cannot be implemented effectively at the continental level. This is dependent on intense cooperation and coordination between the AU Commission and the sub-regional organizations' decision-making organs. Currently, the level of coordination between the AU and RECs/RMs has registered some progress, especially in getting the ASF and CEWS operational as opposed to the other three components of APSA. This could be partly attributed to the existence of a roadmap for the first two components which provides a more structured basis for their becoming operational (Peace and Security Council 2010). While horizontal coordination is envisaged, especially among the regional organizations, there appears to be very little, if any, among the APSA structures. As a result, the AU Commission needs to provide more strategic leadership to the regional organizations in the continued institutionalization of APSA.

UN and APSA

The UN is the principal body charged with the maintenance of world peace and security. According to the *Supplement to an Agenda for Peace*, 'under the Charter, the Security Council has and will continue to have the primary responsibility for maintaining international peace and security' (UN 1995). However, according to the UN Charter, nothing 'precludes the existence of regional arrangements or agencies for dealing with such matters relating to the maintenance of international peace and security as are appropriate for regional action, provided that such arrangements or agencies and their activities are consistent with the Purposes and Principles of the United Nations' (Art. 52.1). These regional or sub-regional agencies have been given the task to 'make every effort to achieve pacific settlement of local disputes through such regional arrangements or by such regional agencies before referring them to the Security Council' (Art. 52.2) (UN 1945). While the continent's engagement in peace and security with the UN dates back to the OAU, it has however intensified in the recent past especially owing to the UN's failures in the face of some of Africa's most profound security challenges including the genocide in Rwanda, the DRC, Burundi, Liberia, Ivory Coast, and the conflict in Somalia.

With the establishment of the PSC which closely mirrors the UN Security Council, AU has been able to authorize deployment with the backing and support from the UN to various trouble spots on the continent. In 2003, the PSC ordered the deployment of AU's first peace operation; the African Union Mission in Burundi (AMIB). In 2004, the UN took over its leadership. In 2007, the African Union-United Nations Hybrid Operation in Darfur was formed. This is one of the most visible AU/UN security partnerships on the continent.

The UN/AU partnership has also grown in other fields, especially capacity building, funding and support of the latter's peace and security activities. However, while the partnership continues to grow, there are still fundamental misconceptions, misunderstandings and misperceptions of its nature, precisely because there are no clear guiding policies and principles. There is therefore a need for a more institutionalized strategic cooperation that recognizes their shared goals and clearly spells out the type, nature and division of responsibilities for the success of their peace support activities.

European Union and APSA

A fully functioning APSA is also largely dependent on external multilateral and bilateral support. This support is delivered through frameworks such as the European Union's (EU) Africa Peace Facility (APF) and the UN's ten-year Capacity-building Programme. To date, the EU has provided the most significant external financial support to APSA. In 2005, it adopted its African Strategy which partly aims to support the achievement of the UN Millennium Development Goals (MDG) on the continent. This strategy recognizes the central role of peace and security in achieving development goals and commits the EU to supporting the development of APSA (Middleton 2008). It is a strategy that also complements the Joint Africa-EU strategy with its three pillars based on security: encouraging dialogue on challenges to peace and security; supporting APSA; and funding AU-led peace support operations. As part of the Joint Africa-EU strategy, the EU established the Africa Peace Facility (APF) in 2004 in response to a request by African leaders at the AU 2003 Maputo summit. Initially, the fund provided a grant worth €250 million for a three-year period to support peace, security and development. Although the programme was intended to be a short-term measure when it ended in 2007, it was renewed till 2010 with the infusion of another €300 million (Mpyisi 2009). The EU support has greatly aided the operational aspects of APSA by providing funding and other non-monetary support to the AU and the regional organizations.

The G8 and APSA

The G8 leaders at successive summits have recognized that peace is an essential condition for sustainable development in Africa and pledged to support initiatives in the prevention, management and resolution of conflicts on the continent. In support of APSA, the G8 have focused, in particular, on supporting the continent's efforts to develop its capacity to undertake peace support operations and peace building initiatives. Issues of peace and security have been a focus of various summits and of declarations adopted at these events.

At the Kananaskis summit of 2002, the G8 adopted an African Action Plan containing a detailed list of commitments including to 'provide technical and financial assistance so that, by 2010, African countries and regional and sub-regional organizations are able to engage more effectively to prevent and resolve violent conflict on the continent, and undertake peace support operations in accordance with the United Nations Charter' (OECD 2008). In 2003, the Evian summit followed up on the earlier pledge with the 'Joint Africa/G8 Action Plan to enhance African Capabilities to undertake Peace Support Operations' (G8 2004). At the Sea Island summit of June 2004, the G8 adopted an 'Action Plan for Expanding Global Capacity for Peace Support Operations' (G8 2004). Among several other action points, the Group pledged to train and, where appropriate, equip a total of 75,000 troops worldwide by 2010, in line with the commitments undertaken at the previous two summits. They further pledged that this effort would have a sustained focus on Africa and other nations that could contribute to peace support operations both in Africa and elsewhere. The Heiligendamm summit in 2007 agreed to strengthen the civilian component of the ASF, including its police capabilities. Although there were no new pledges made at the Hokkaido summit of 2008 in northern Japan, the Group reiterated their commitment to promoting peace on the African continent by enhancing its peacekeeping capabilities through support offered to APSA and ASF (Hubbard 2008).

Other partners that have helped to operationalize APSA include India, China and individual member countries of the G8 and the European Union. In recognition of its primary responsibility to maintain peace and security in the world, the UN has variously supported AU peace and security endeavours, including APSA.

Civil Society and APSA

The AU's Constitutive Act gives considerable prominence to the role of civil society in the AU's activities. Articles 5 and 22 provide for the creation of the Economic, Social and Cultural Council (ECOSOCC) as an 'advisory organ composed of different social and professional groups of the member states of the Union'. Unfortunately, the evolution of the security architecture as well as the development of the AU has largely been intergovernmental processes. Civil society organizations (CSOs) on the continent are yet to seize their rightful place as provided for in the Constitutive Act for several reasons. Currently, CSOs are struggling with basic challenges around a number of key issues. First, there is a lack of trust between the organizations and governments that are often reluctant to recognize them as professionals and, instead, treat CSOs apprehensively as unwanted watchdogs. Secondly, there is lack of requisite human capacity among civil society organizations as most people leave their countries especially due to an unfavourable working environment, join government or are recruited by international organizations or donor agencies. Another challenge facing civil societies is lack of funding which makes them dependent on external donors (Klingebiel et al 2008).

Lack of predictable and independent funding has especially had a negative impact on the development of civil society on the continent. It is only organizations from South Africa that have had the resources to engage with continental issues including those of peace and security. Organizations from other countries, in spite of their vibrancy, are mostly dedicated and confined to local challenges and cannot therefore contribute effectively to the AU's peace and security agenda.

Nevertheless, because there is already space for CSO engagement with the AU, it is only a matter of time before competent and continent-wide organizations, capable of engaging with the peace and security agenda evolve.

Conclusion

In the face of the UN's failure to act effectively in some of Africa's most serious security challenges – including the genocide in Rwanda, conflicts in the DRC, Burundi, Liberia, Ivory Coast and Somalia – the AU is increasingly actively pursuing an agenda for continental peace and stability. This re-vitalization of the defunct OAU through AU also coincided with a paradigm shift on the continent, dubbed the 'African Renaissance'. In the on-going peace and security discourse, the slogan 'African solutions to African problems' has taken centre stage. Among other leaders, this new thinking was popularized by Thabo Mbeki, the then President of South Africa, who actively supported institutions that advocated Pan Africanism. These institutions included, *inter alia,* the African Union, the Pan African Parliament and the New Partnership for African Development (NEPAD).

'African solutions to African problems' reflects the justifiable need for greater African responsibility, autonomy and the imperative to develop indigenous conflict prevention and management capacities in the face of international indifference or at times unhealthy interference in certain African conflicts (Ayangafac and Cilliers 2009). However, African or local ownership in developing and implementing policy options is not synonymous with and should not be used as an excuse for international disengagement or desertion. After all, international actors and interests have been at the heart of Africa's conflicts through much of its history.

Within the context of 'African solutions to African problems', the current trend where there is very high reliance financially on international partners to operationalize APSA is worrying. This trend is observable not just at the AU level but also within regional organizations and associated centres of excellence where training is undertaken. This overreliance invariably undermines the principle of ownership and also raises questions of sustainability, predictability and agenda setting. As is naturally expected and as part of lessons learnt from the past, no international assistance is ever interest-free, and rarely is the interest altruistic international peace and security.

As a way of ensuring that Africans own and drive the agenda to operationalize APSA, the AU must ensure that it develops mechanisms, not only by diversifying partner support but also, crucially, by ensuring that a sizeable proportion of its budget is derived from its member states. In this regard, the case of ECOWAS is worth replicating both by AU and at the level of other regional organizations. Through a resource mobilization strategy by members, ECOWAS has instituted a Community Levy, a percentage of which is dedicated to the ECOWAS Peace Fund. The West African economic community accounts for approximately 80% of the budget to support its conflict prevention and management endeavours. As such, it is not dependent on partner support for its programmes and only regards it (partner support) as value addition. This has made its peace fund flexible and even enabled it to respond to member states' national peace and security challenges, including anti-corruption activities (Peace and Security Council 2010).

The AU should also ensure that the conceptualization and operationalization of APSA is flexible enough to respond to current and emerging threats. Emerging security challenges such as terrorism, piracy and the need to improve the governance of security forces in member states currently fall outside the ambit of the ASF. A related challenge which a fully functioning APSA has to contend with rests with the very genesis of the security challenges on the continent: the nature of the African state. The state still remains an alien entity to the majority of its citizens and is unable to guarantee the minimum requirements of statehood. While, currently, there is an overemphasis in terms of peace and security support on the components of APSA especially from the EU, the biggest partner, it should be recognized that state fragility remains the biggest source of insecurity in Africa. Therefore, greater emphasis must be placed on nurturing and strengthening democratic institutions at all levels from national and regional to the AU level.

Ultimately, for peace and security to be a reality in Africa, Africans must set and own the agenda, with support from the international community to ensure proper functioning of APSA. Anything short of this roadmap will relegate APSA to the backwaters, which several other well-intentioned but inappropriately conceptualized and executed initiatives have suffered.

References

African Union Peace Support Operations Division, 2010, *Report of the 4th Annual African Standby Force Training Implementation Workshop,* Harare, African Union.

African Union, 2002, *Protocol Relating to the Establishment of the Peace and Security Council of the African Union,* Durban, African Union.

African Union, 2007, *Modalities for the Functioning of the Panel of the Wise as Adopted by the Peace and Security Council at its 100th Meeting,* Addis Ababa, African Union.

African Union, 2007, *Memorandum of Understanding on Cooperation in the Area of Peace and Security between the African Union, the Regional Economic Communities and the Coordinating Mechanism of the Regional Standby Brigades of Eastern Africa and Northern Africa,* Addis Ababa, African Union.

Amoo, Sam, 1993, 'The Role of the OAU: Past, Present and Future', in *Making War and Waging Peace: Foreign Intervention in Africa,* D. Smock, ed., Washington DC, United States Institute for Peace Press.

Aning, Kwesi, 2008, *The African Union's Peace and Security Architecture: Defining an Emerging Response Mechanism,* Uppsala, the Nordic African Institute.

Ayangafac, Chrysantus and Cilliers, Jakkie, 2009, *African solutions to African problems: in Search of the African Renaissance,* Pretoria: Institute for Security Studies, Accessed on 2 February 2011 http://www.iss.co.za/iss_today.php?ID=1163.

Daley, Patricia, 2006, 'Challenges to Peace: Conflict Resolution in the Great Lakes Region of Africa', *Third World Quarterly,* 27:1360-2241.

Dersso, Solomon, 2010, *The Role and Place of the African Standby Force within the African Peace and Security Architecture,* Nairobi, Institute for Security Studies.

Francis, David, 2007, *Uniting Africa: Building Regional Peace and Security Systems*, Hampshire, Ashgate Publishing Limited.

G8, 2004, *G8 Action Plan: Exploring Global Capability for Peace Support Operations,* Sea Island. Accessed 5 February 2011, http://www.g8.utoronto.ca/summit/2004seaisland/index.html.

Heinlein, Peter, 2007, *AU Launches 'Panel of the Wise*, VOA News, 18 December 2007, Accessed 3 February 2011, http://www.voanews.com/english/.

Hubbard, Ben, 2011, *The 2008 G8 Summit: Outcomes for Africa,* Accessed 20 January 2011. http://www.g8summit.go.jp/eng/doc/index.html.

Kimathi, Leah, 2010, *A Common Agenda of Post Conflict Reconstruction among Eastern Africa's Sub-Regional Organizations: Exploring the Challenges*, Nairobi, International Peace Support Training Centre.

Kioko, Ben, 2003, 'The Right of Intervention under the African Union's Constitutive Act', *International Review of the Red Cross,* 85: 807-825.

Klingebiel, Stephan et al., 2008, *Donor Contribution to the Strengthening of the African Peace and Security Architecture*, Bonn, German Development Institute.

Middleton, R., *The EU and the African Peace and Security Architecture,* Accessed 10 February 2011 www.chathamhouse.org.uk/publications/papers/view/-/id/625/

Mpyisi, Kenneth, 2009, *How EU Support of the African Peace and Security Architecture Impacts Democracy Building and Human Security Enhancement in Africa*, Stockholm, International Institute for Democracy and Electoral Assistance.

Mwanasali, Musifiky, 2003, 'From the Organization of African Unity to the African Union', in *From Cape to Congo, Southern Africa's Evolving Security Challenges,* M. Baregu, and C. Landsberg, eds, Colorado, Lynne Rienner.

Olonisakin, Fumi and Ero, C., 2003, 'Africa and the Regionalization of Peace Operations', in *The United Nations and Regional Security: Europe and Beyond,* M. Pugh, and W. Sidh, eds, Colorado, Lynne Rienner.

Oloo, Adams, 2008, 'Regional Institutions and the Quest for Security in the Horn of Africa', in *Human Security: Setting the Agenda for the Horn of Africa,* Makumi Mwagiru, ed., Nairobi, Africa Peace Forum.

Peace and Security Council (AU), 2010, *African Peace and Security Architecture: 2010 Assessment Study,* Addis Ababa, African Union.

Powell, Katrina, 2005, *The African Union's Emerging Peace and Security Regime: Opportunities and Challenges for Delivering on the Responsibility to Protect,* Ontario, The North-South Institute, Accessed 8 January 2011, http://www.nsi-ins.ca/english/research/progress/19.asp.

4

Regional Financial Integration: Evidence from Stock Markets in the West African Monetary Zone

Terfa Williams Abraham

Introduction

One of the unresolved issues facing Africa in the twenty-first century is the challenge posed by achieving stronger integration. The challenge for the Economic Community of West Africa States (ECOWAS) sub-region is of particular interest due to its heterogeneous socio-cultural and economic characteristic and the need to achieve a monetary union. While efforts have focused on migration and accelerating direct trade links (see Njinkeu 2009), regional integration could be enhanced through other channels as well. Thus, the need to explore further channels to accelerate the pace of integration cannot be overemphasized.

To achieve stronger integration and economic union within the ECOWAS sub-region, the West African Monetary Zone (WAMZ) was established in 2000 to harmonize the macroeconomic policies of its member countries. A merger is anticipated between the WAMZ and the West African Economic and Monetary Union (UEMOA) once the WAMZ becomes a single monetary zone. At present, WAMZ member countries are the Gambia, Ghana, Guinea, Liberia, Nigeria and Sierra Leone. Among these countries, Nigeria and Ghana have very sizeable stock markets. The integration of both stock markets and the implication it holds for integration in the sub-region, however, has not been given adequate attention in the literature.

The integration of financial markets has been argued to have the potential to enhance economic integration (see Ogun and Adenikinju 1992; Kim and Singal 2000; Agathee 2008). Others like Harris (2008) have also argued that market efficiency is likely to increase with greater integration. While the evidence around these issues is mixed, providing further evidence from the WAMZ, would be useful to the debate on how to enhance regional integration in the ECOWAS sub-region.

The objective of this chapter, therefore, is to test for the efficiency of stock markets in the WAMZ and, also, to examine if they are co-integrated. If the markets were efficient and co-integrated, it would imply that their integration would improve their efficiency, which would in turn enhance regional integration (Harris 2008). On the other hand, if they were efficient and not co-integrated, it would imply that the markets would be better off not being integrated and, hence, would hamper regional integration; as it would not be desirable for national government to pursue policies of achieving integrated financial markets within the sub-region.

The chapter is arranged into five sections. Section one is the introduction which highlights the research problem, gap from the literature and objectives of the chapter. Section two presents the conceptualization and reviews-related empirical and theoretical literature. The research methodology is discussed in section three, while the results from data analysis are discussed in section four. Lastly, the summary and conclusion are presented in section five.

Literature Review

Conceptualization

There is a close link between the concepts of regional and economic integration. The concept of economic integration generally refers to growing economic ties among countries, while regional integration extends to public sector activity, such as the coordination of economic policies (Ogun and Adenikinju 1992). In relation to financial markets, integration refers to a process of unifying markets and enabling convergence of risk-adjusted returns on the assets of similar maturity across the markets (Harris 2008).

Recently, and coupled with the wave of globalization, there has been a shift from bank–based capital market development to a more holistic approach that aims at globalizing the securities' market as well as other financial institutions with banks (Kim and Singal 2000). One reason that makes capital markets the focal point of the shifting emphasis, as argued by Popiel (1990), is their ability to mobilize long-term savings for financing entrepreneurs, encourage broader ownership of firms and improve the efficiency of resource allocation through competitive pricing mechanism. Demirguc-kunt and Levine (1996) also argued that apart from these primary benefits, globalizing stock markets would ensure efficient financial intermediation, bring further gains to the various economies and also bring about a shift from debt to equity financing across countries (see Tella and Adesoye 2008).

Stock market Integration is generally seen as beneficial as it increases the probability to attract inward portfolio investment, boost domestic savings and improve the pricing and availability of capital for domestic investment (Jefferis 1995; Kenny and Moss 1998). Integration of stock markets, however, could also bring about increased exposure of countries to increased vulnerability and external shocks, which could hamper desired benefits from integration (see Kim and Singal 2000; and AfDB 2008). Further complications could include exchange and interest rates volatility and strong capital outflows which could have adverse effect on economic growth.

On efficiency, there are three variants: the Weak form (when security prices reflect all information found in past prices and volume); the Semi-strong form (when security prices reflect all publicly available information); and Strong form (when security prices reflect all public and private information). These components constitute the efficient market hypothesis: a theory that argues that capital markets are efficient in reflecting information about individual stocks and about the stock market as a whole (Fama 1965). The least form of efficiency is the weak form, and is the aspect considered in this chapter.

Empirical Literature

Since the early 1990s, studies (e.g., Ogun and Adenikinju 1992) have noted that of all the groups in the world, Africans trade the least with each other. And despite the establishment of economic communities at the sub-region, more efforts needed to be made to accelerate the pace of integration. Though their study related more to trade unions, they concluded that Africa stood to gain if markets were integrated. And so, in providing evidence on the role of markets in enhancing growth, Rousseau and Wachtel (1999) examined the relationship between equity markets and economic growth in Africa using the vector auto-regression model. The panel data covered 47 countries, including Nigeria, from 1980 to 1995. It was found out that the stock market promotes economic performance by providing an exit mechanism to venture capitalists; offers liquidity to investors that encourages international diversification and portfolio flows; and provides firms with access to permanent capital which can then be placed in large, indivisible projects.

In a different study, Kim and Singal (2000) investigated the effect of market opening on stock market returns, volatility and market efficiency for selected emerging markets. The study covered 27 countries, including Nigeria, and employed autoregressive conditional heteroskedasticity (ARCH) and generalized autoregressive conditional heteroskedasticity (GARCH) models for analysis. The study found out that stock returns increase immediately after market opening but tend to decrease subsequently.

Agathee (2008) tested for interdependence between the Mauritian stock market and six African equity markets, namely Botswana, Malawi, Namibia, South Africa, Zambia and Zimbabwe, using weekly stock market indexes from January 2000 to September 2007. From the Granger causality test used for analysis, it was found out that there was a unidirectional causality between Zimbabwe and Mauritius. This implies that, short-term movements from the Zimbabwean stock exchange were likely to influence the short-term performance of the Mauritian stock exchange. Though the results for others were not significant, the Johansen co-integration tests showed that there was a co-integrating relationship between Mauritius and the selected stock markets. In a study on the determinants of savings in Nigeria, Nwachukwu and Egwaikhide (2007) noted that the error correction model could also be very useful in estimating co-integration relationships.

The African Development Bank (AfDB) in its 2008 report presented a cross-sectional analysis on regional financial institutions (RFIs) in three sub-regions: the Common Market for Eastern and Southern Africa (COMESA), the Arab Maghreb Union (UMA), and Central African Economic and Monetary Community (CEMAC). Relying on that report, this section highlights the progress of regional integration in the selected regions.

The long-term objective for COMESA is to create a single market in financial services to support its regional integration. Though progress was made in modernizing national financial institutions, the overall conclusion from the report was that COMESA was still lagging behind in achieving financial integration. The objective of the UMA (Arab Maghreb Union comprising Algeria, Morocco, Tunisia, Mauritania and Libya, established by a Treaty in 1989) is to establish a free trade agreement (FTA), harmonize customs duties and regulations, and ultimately create a Common Market. The UMA anchored its financial integration on the following: the harmonization of monetary and fiscal policies, financial and legal regulations, supervisory systems, and monetary systems (AfDB 2008). These efforts were to be complemented by the creation of a common bank (i.e., the Bank of Maghreb) for investments and trade. However, the financial sector of the UMA had not been achieved as expected.

The core objective of CEMAC is to create a Common Market. Among other measures, this would be achieved by promoting regional economic and financial integration among its member states. However, the financial system of CEMAC is still relatively underdeveloped, insufficiently diversified, and dominated by the banking sector. It is also unevenly distributed among member states, with nearly one-third of the banks located in Cameroon. The banking sector also holds over 85 per cent of financial assets and liabilities, while the non-bank financial sector is small and operates almost exclusively at the national level.

In summary, the overall assessment in the report was that the progress in RFIs in the regions had been slow and had to be accelerated. The reasons for the slow progress was attributed to: divergent macroeconomic situations and an uneven level of bank soundness across member countries; a lack of political commitment to RFI; a lack of adequate capacities (human and financial); overambitious and ill-defined objectives and time frames; weak regional institutions charged with managing the integration process; lack of coordination between national and regional strategies; and conflicting regional obligations due to multi-organization membership of some countries.

Theoretical Issues

As noted in Harris (2008), there is considerable evidence that both stock markets and banks contribute to long-run economic growth. The argument, according to Harris, however, is that the efficiency of a stock market could be higher in the context of a regional financial centre than when concentrated to serve a specific country. Thus, measuring integration and efficiency is therefore important for ascertaining the benefit of integration. The degree of financial market integration, however, can be measured using different approaches and there is no widespread agreement about a particular measure (Baele *et al* 2004). For instance, Walti (2006) argued that while the *de jure* approach measurement of financial market integration relies on the implementation of liberalization policies on financial markets, the *de facto* measure focuses on the outcomes of such liberalization, the volume of equity flows, foreign direct investment, and on the return on asset prices.

There are also other methods for measuring integration such as using correlation index, autoregressive distributed lag model, Vector autoregressive model, Augmented Engle granger co-integration tests, error correction model, among others (Alagidede 2008). Though these methods have their strengths and weaknesses, the error correction model has the advantage of measuring the short and long-run relationship connecting two or more variables in a single equation.

Similarly, while efficiency can be tested econometrically using various models, it is premised on the theoretical work of Fama (1965): the efficient market hypothesis (EMH). The EMH has three variants: the weak form, the semi-strong form and the strong form. The weak form, however, offers the theoretical framework to test for efficiency in this paper because of its simplicity which can be expressed in a simple random walk model. The weak-form efficiency is represented as

$$P_t = P_{t-1} + \text{Expected return} + \text{random error } t \text{——————————— (2.1)}$$

Where P_t is the current stock market prices and P_{t-1} is its lagged value following an AR(1) process. Since stock prices only respond to *new* information, which by definition arrives randomly, stock prices are said to follow a random walk. The next section describes how these methods were estimated and the data collected.

Research Methodology

Stock market data for Nigeria and Ghana were collected daily on a 5-day-weekbasis from 5 November 2007 to 3 July 2009 from African Business Research Limited (ABRL). The choice of this period enables the analysis to provide findings that would give insight on stock market efficiency and integration within the context of the recent global financial crisis. Ghana and Nigeria were selected because they are the major stock markets in the WAMZ sub-region.

Following Fama (1965), the weak form efficient market hypothesis was used as the theoretical framework for efficiency; hence, the autoregressive model of order one (AR,1) was used for the estimation. The model is presented below:

$$NSE_t = á_1 + á_2 NSE_{t-1} + e_{t1} \qquad (3.1)$$
$$GSE_t = â_0 + â_1 GSE_{t-1} + e_{t2} \qquad (3.2)$$

Where NSE_{t-1} and GSE_{t-1}, are the previous values of the Nigerian and Ghanaian stock market prices respectively.

For the co-integrating relationship, error correction model (ECM) adapted from Nwachukwu and Egwaikhide (2007) was employed because of its strength in providing estimates for short-run and long-run relationship in a single equation. The model is specified below:

$$\text{«NSE}_t = \acute{a}_0 + c(\text{NSE}_{t-1} - n_2\text{GSE}_{t-1}) + n_1\text{»GSE}_t + \hat{\imath}_t \rule{3cm}{0.4pt} \quad (3.3)$$

Where $\hat{\imath}_t$ is the residual term and H is a symbol used to denote first difference of the variables. The coefficient c, has an *a priori* expectation of a negative sign and is used to test for long-run equilibrium between the NSE and the GSE. On the other hand, the coefficient, n_1, shows the short-run equilibrium connecting both variables. The study raised two hypotheses. They are specified in their null form below:

Hypothesis One:
H_o: stock markets in the WAMZ are not efficient
Hypothesis Two:
H_1: stock markets in the WAMZ are not integrated

Equation 3.1 and 3.2 were used to test the first hypothesis for Nigeria and Ghana respectively, while equation 3.3 was used to test the second hypothesis.

Figure 1: Trend of Nigerian and Ghanaian Stock Exchanges: 2007 - 2009

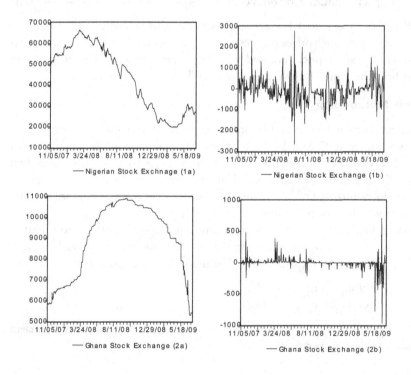

Results and Discussions

The trends of the Ghanaian and Nigerian stock markets for the sample period are presented in Figure 1. The trend to the left shows movement of both stock markets while the trend to the right shows their frequency.

The left trends shows that the Nigerian stock market witnessed a quick rise in the early period but declined slowly over the sample period, while the Ghanaian stock market increased slowly then declined faster within the same period. In the right hand side, the Nigerian stock market exhibited higher frequency and spikes across the sample period, unlike the Ghanaian stock market that exhibited high frequency at certain periods only. This trend implies that the Nigerian stock exchange was more vulnerable to the crisis as well as to domestic issues, while the Ghanaian stock market was less vulnerable.

To estimate the models, it is required that a unit root test be conducted to ascertain stationarity of the variables. The result shows that both variables are stationary at first difference; which is a requirement for estimating error correction model with two variables. The stationarity result is presented in the Appendix.

Test of Hypotheses: Test for Efficiency
The result for test of efficiency in Nigerian stock exchange is presented in Table 1.

Table 1: Weak Form Efficient Market Hypothesis (EMH) - NIGERIA

Dependent Variable: NSE

Method: Least Squares

Sample(adjusted): 11/07/2007 7/03/2009

Included observations: 433 after adjusting endpoints

Variable	Coefficient	Std. Error	t-Statistic	Prob.
C	-0.000353	0.000279	-1.263436	0.2071
NSE(-1)	0.453448	0.042905	10.56863	0.0000
R-squared	0.205817	Mean dependent var		-0.000634
Adjusted R-squared	0.203974	S.D. dependent var		0.006487
S.E. of regression	0.005788	Akaike info criterion		-7.461522
Sum squared resid	0.014438	Schwarz criterion		-7.442719
Log likelihood	1617.419	F-statistic		111.6958
Durbin-Watson stat	2.145387	Prob (F-statistic)		0.000000

Source: Eviews Output (Researchers Estimation)

The probabilities for the t and f statistic values are significant as they are less than one per cent. This implies rejection of the null hypothesis while the alternative is accepted, indicating that the Nigerian stock exchange is weak form efficient. On the other hand, the result for the weak form efficiency test of the Ghanaian stock exchange is presented in Table 2.

Table 2: Weak Form Efficient Market Hypothesis (EMH) - Ghana

Dependent Variable: GSE

Method: Least Squares

Sample(adjusted): 11/07/2007 7/03/2009

Included observations: 433 after adjusting endpoints

Variable	Coefficient	Std. Error	t-Statistic	Prob.
C	-8.79E-05	0.000292	-0.301414	0.7632
GSE(-1)	-0.170326	0.047464	-3.588498	0.0004
R-squared	0.029011	Mean dependent var		-7.52E-05
Adjusted R-squared	0.026758	S.D. dependent var		0.006151
S.E. of regression	0.006068	Akaike info criterion		-7.366838
Sum squared resid	0.015872	Schwarz criterion		-7.348036
Log likelihood	1596.920	F-statistic		12.87732
Durbin-Watson stat	1.999362	Prob(F-statistic)		0.000371

Source: Eviews Output (Researchers Estimation)

Likewise, the t and f statistics are significant as their probability values are below one per cent. Thus, the null hypothesis is rejected while the alternative is accepted, implying that the Ghanaian stock exchange is also weak form efficient. Empirical evidence, therefore, supports that the WAMZ stock markets are weak form efficient. Therefore, it is expected that their efficiency will increase if both markets are integrated. Evidence of no integration would thus imply that, the efficiency of both markets would not be sustained if they were integrated. This brings us to the test of the second hypothesis.

Test of Hypotheses: Test for Co-integration
The error correction model result is presented in Table 3.

Table 3: Error Correction Model Result

Dependent Variable: D(NSE)

Method: Least Squares

Sample(adjusted): 11/06/2007 7/03/2009

Included observations: 434 after adjusting endpoints

Variable	Coefficient	Std. Error	t-Statistic	Prob.
C	-0.000622	0.000312	-1.993790	0.0468
RES(-1)	-0.001518	0.001892	-0.802318	0.4228
D(GSE)	0.007579	0.052042	0.145624	0.8843
R-squared	0.001493	Mean dependent var		-0.000623
Adjusted R-squared	-0.003140	S.D. dependent var		0.006483
S.E. of regression	0.006494	Akaike info criterion		-7.229135
Sum squared resid	0.018173	Schwarz criterion		-7.200980
Log likelihood	1571.722	F-statistic		0.322308
Durbin-Watson stat	1.092696	Prob(F-statistic)		0.724649

Source: Eviews Output (Researcher's Estimation)

The short-run coefficient *(D(GSE))* is positive but not significant. This implies that, the NSE and GSE are likely to respond in the same direction to short-run shocks. Though the result is statistically significant, the extent of response would, however, depend on their size and other domestic factors. On the other hand, the long-run coefficient *(RES(-1))* has the expected *a priori* negative sign, but is also not significant. This implies that though there is the tendency for the NSE and the GSE to be co-integrated (be at equilibrium in the long run), distortions in the short run are not likely to be corrected in the long run to bring about integration. Thus, the null of the second hypothesis is accepted while the alternative is rejected, implying that, stock markets in the WAMZ are not integrated.

Summary and Conclusion

The conclusion to be drawn from this chapter is that though stock markets in the WAMZ are efficient in the weak form, they are not integrated. This implies that while the integration of markets is necessary to enhance regional financial integration, the WAMZ stock markets would become less efficient if integrated; hence, it would be better to operate both markets as separate entities. Another implication is that investors would prefer to invest in both markets as separate markets and would not like to invest if the markets were integrated. Therefore, the integration of financial markets would not be likely to bring about the desired increased integration in the sub-region as the benefits from investing in such markets would not be likely to be sustained if the markets are integrated. Thus, policies need to be put in place to ensure that WAMZ member countries tilt the operation of the financial markets towards integration and in addressing the factors that limit the efficient operation of their capital markets so as to enhance the pace of regional integration in the ECOWAS sub-region.

References

AfDB, 2008, 'Financial Sector Integration in Three Regions of Africa: How Regional Financial Integration Can Support Growth, Development and Poverty Reduction', African Development Bank (AfDB) Report on Making Africa Work.

Agathee, U.S., 2008, 'Interdependence of the Stock Exchange of Mauritius with Selected African Stock Markets: An Empirical Study', A Paper Presented at the EABR & TLC Conferences Proceedings Rothenburg, Germany.

Alagidede, P., 2008, 'African Stock Market Integration: Implications for Portfolio Diversification and International Risk Sharing', Proceedings of the African Economic Conference 2008, pp. 25-54.

Baele, L., Ferrando, A., Hordahl, P., Krylova, E. and Monnet, C. 2004, 'Measuring Financial Integration in the Euro Area', European Central Bank Occasional Paper 14.

Demirguc-Kunt, A. and Levine, R., 1996, 'Stock Market Development and Financial Intermediaries: Stylized Facts', *The World Bank Economic Review,* 10(2).

Fama, E., 1965, 'The Behaviour of Stock Market Prices', *The Journal of Business,* Vol. 38 (January), 34-105.

Harris, L., 2008, 'Regional Integration and Capital Markets in Africa', A publication of the African Economic Research Consortium (AERC), in *Financial Systems and Monetary Policy in Africa,* Mthuli Ncube, ed., pp. 89-101.

Jefferis, K., 1995, 'The Development of Stock Markets in Sub-Saharan Africa', *South Africa Journal of Economics,* 63.

Kenny, C. and Moss, T., 1998, 'Stock Markets in Africa: Emerging Lion or White Elephants', *World Development,* 26.

Kim, E.H. and Singal, V., 2000, 'Stock Market Openings: Experience of Emerging Economies', *University of Chicago Journal of Business,* Vol. 73, No. 1.

Njinkeu, D., 2009, 'Intra-African Trade and Regional Integration', A Publication of the African Development Bank (AfDB) in *Accelerating Africa's Development Five Years into the 21ˢᵗ Century,* pp. 247-272.

Nwachukwu, T.E. and Egwaikhide, F.O., 2007, 'An Error-Correction Model of the Determinants of Private Saving in Nigeria', A Paper presented at the African Economic Society (AES) Conference, Cape Town, South Africa, July.

Ogun, O. and Adenikinju, A., 1992, 'Integrating the African Region: Lessons from Historical Experiences', A paper presented at the Nigerian Economic Society (NES) 1992 Annual Conference.

Popiel, P.A., 1990, 'Developing Financial Markets in Sub-Saharan Africa', EDI Working Papers Washington D.C.: The World Bank.

Rousseau, P.L. and Wachtel, P., 1999, 'Equity Markets and Growth: Cross-Country Evidence on Timing and Outcomes, 1980-1995', A paper presented at the 1998 meetings of American Economic Association and Society.

Tella, S.A. and Adesoye, B., 2008, 'Internationalisation of Africa's stock markets: prospects and Challenges', A paper presented at the Department of Economics, Olabisi Onabanjo University, Ogun State.

Walti, Sebastien, 2006, 'Stock market synchronisation and monetary integration', A publication of the National Centre of Competence in Research (NCCR) supported by the Swiss National Science Foundation.

Appendix

1: Stationarity Test Results

(Ai) NSE At Levels

ADF Test Statistic	0.081291	1% Critical Value*	-3.4476
		5% Critical Value	-2.8685
		10% Critical Value	-2.5704

*MacKinnon critical values for rejection of hypothesis of a unit root.

Augmented Dickey-Fuller Test Equation

(Aii) NSE At First Difference

ADF Test Statistic	-12.73863	1% Critical Value*	-3.4476
		5% Critical Value	-2.8685
		10% Critical Value	-2.5704

*MacKinnon critical values for rejection of hypothesis of a unit root.

Augmented Dickey-Fuller Test Equation

(Bi) GSE At Levels

ADF Test Statistic	-0.166764	1% Critical Value*	-3.4476
		5% Critical Value	-2.8685
		10% Critical Value	-2.5704

*MacKinnon critical values for rejection of hypothesis of a unit root.

Augmented Dickey-Fuller Test Equation

(Bii) GSE At Firdt Difference

ADF Test Statistic	-24.65698	1% Critical Value*	-3.4476
		5% Critical Value	-2.8685
		10% Critical Value	-2.5704

*MacKinnon critical values for rejection of hypothesis of a unit root.

Augmented Dickey-Fuller Test Equation

Sources: Eviews Output (Researchers Estimation)

5

Gender Dimensions of Informal Cross-border Trade in the West African Sub-region (ECOWAS) Borders

Olabisi S. Yusuff

Introduction

Formal and informal cross-border trade in West Africa has increased since the 1990s because of economic liberalization policies, population growth and urbanization. This expansion has been credited with deepening regional integration, improving economic growth and benefiting the population through employment, market and product diversification, increased outlets for goods produced and manufactured in the region and improvements in food availability (Morris and Saul 2000). It has been suggested that trade in non-traditional exports in agricultural products like livestock, fish, handicrafts and manufactured goods will increasingly drive sustained economic growth in West Africa. This implies the importance of strong connections between trade and other sectors of West African economies, particularly agricultural production and processing, fisheries and manufacturing (ECOWAS-WAEMU 2006).

Informal trade is an integral but unrecognized component of Africa's economy. Evidence shows that, on the average, sixty per cent of African trade is informal (Ackello-Ogutu 1998; Morris and Saul 2000). This is because Informal trade in Africa has persisted despite the efforts made to graft it into formal economy in developing countries (Olutayo 2005). Goldberg and Pavenik (2003) define the informal economy as the sector of the economy that does not comply with the labour market legislation and does not provide workers' benefits. Informal trade here means trade that is not recorded officially by customs at borders; but it does not necessarily mean illegal trade.

The history of cross-border trade exchange is tied up with the emergence, about twenty years ago, of floating exchange rates and the Eurobond market

(Chichilinsky 2003). With the current economic and socio-political environment of sub-Saharan Africa, an increasing percentage of the populace seek alternative means of livelihood, some of which are high-risk activities. Oftentime, these alternatives include cross-border trading and migration to neighbouring states (IOM Southern Africa Newsletter 2010).

Cross-border trade cuts across all ages, religion, ethnic groups and gender. The main type of trade practised by women across West African borders is informal cross border trade (ICBT). ICBT plays a vital role in poverty reduction, employment, and income opportunities (Kabira 2006; Cagatay and Ozler 1995). It is a vital source of livelihood for the poor and an important component of Africa's economy, contributing immensely to the economy of Africa, particularly in terms of uplifting women's economic status, and strengthening food security, regional economic trade and social integration (Matsuyama 2011). ICBT does not occur in a vacuum as it takes place within the broader trade and developmental context internationally, regionally and nationally. Informal cross-border traders import essential and scarce commodities into their countries (Mijere 2006). It is revealing that cross-border women traders in West Africa employ one or two people and support an average of 3.2 children, in addition to 3.1 dependants who are not their children or spouses (UNIFEM 2008).

UNIFEM (2008) reports show that women constitute between seventy to eighty per cent of people engaged in cross-border trade and are actively involved in moving goods through border crossing points. However, it should be noted that women had previously been engaged in long-distance trade before this time and had been earning incomes for household support. But in the aftermath of 1980s economic crisis, informal cross-border trade became a safety net for the unemployed in Africa, providing sources of income for those without formal education (Mijere 2006). Importantly, by ignoring women's informal trading activities, African countries are neglecting a significant proportion of their trade.

Ironically, ICBT is often perceived as illegal dealing in stolen and, banned goods, as well as in illegal drugs. This perception has, unfortunately, resulted in most West African countries focusing only on formal international trade with complete disregard of the informal aspects of the trade, despite the significant contributions that the trade makes to the overall national economy. Now, informal cross-border trade is coming under the spotlight in connection with the need to alleviate poverty in general and feminized poverty in particular. For this to happen effectively and efficiently, policy and institutional reforms should create an enabling environment for cross-border women traders. The challenges to free and profitable participation in trade have to be identified and documented. This study therefore draws attention to the circumstances of women traders across West African borders within the context of the evolving policy that must take full cognizance of the situations of women and their small-scale cross- border trade activities. The findings in this study will lay a basis for efforts by individual countries to offer concessionary facilities to women traders so that they can realize their full potential, and ultimately enable them to take advantage of the West African Economic Liberation Policy. This study focuses on women's capacities, their contributions to intra-West African trade, and particularly on cross-border trade and its constraints.

Brief Literature Review and Theoretical Framework

Since the colonial period, West African women have been involved in trade in their own countries and across the borders, particularly in the distribution of food and small consumer items and trade services. Their active involvement in small-scale trade is linked with the gendered construction of the colonial economy and society, which allowed male access to formal education and employment in the colonial bureaucracy and other forms of formal employment.

Tsikata (2009) explains that residential regulations during the colonial period restricted women's access to urban areas and confined them to rural areas under the jurisdiction of chiefs. These circumstances resulted in the gender segmentation of the labour force, which forced women to restrict themselves to the margins of the colonial order, delivering much- needed services to male migrants and establishing themselves in the informal distribution of goods and services. These colonial patterns have persisted into post-colonial period, reinforced by continuing gender discrimination in terms of access to education and formal employment and growing informalization of work due to economic liberalization policies.

Many women have entered the informal economy due to the dearth of opportunities for them. Women traders have used global economic openings to become cross-border traders. Traditionally, women cross-border traders were engaged in the sale of unprocessed and processed food such as fish, salt and foodstuffs. Because of the segmentation of labour in production and distribution, men and women have traded in distinct products in the market places (Economic Commission for Africa 2010). Originally, women were confined to jobs such as food selling and shop assistance in businesses at border crossings; they are now involved in cross-border trade, involving a range of goods and services, which has resulted in new transnational networks, supported by commonalities in language, culture and kinship system (Economic Commission for Africa 2010).

Women cross-border traders (WCBTs) are now more diverse and engage in higher value and volume of goods than the traditional sale of a few items every market day (Morris and Saul 2000). WCBTs trade in agricultural processed goods and light manufacturing commodities (Muzvidiziwa 1998). Cross-border trade has enabled many women to become financially independent (Desai 2009). Many female household heads are out of poverty through cross-border trading (Muzvidziwa 1998). Many women opted for cross-border trade as a strategy to ease competition and cope with poverty (Shamu 2005).

The WCBT path is strewn with difficulties and danger (Kabira 2006) as ICBT is a risky business for women (Matsuyama 2011). WCBTs are open to economic and personal risks such as robbery and harassment (Ishwawe 2010). According to Matsuyama (2011), WCBTs do not benefit from preferential tariffs, and face risks

of abuse, harassment, exploitation and exposure to extreme vulnerability. They are
vulnerable to various health risks. Despite these facts, WCBTs make huge
contributions to Africa's economy, but they are neglected by mainstream trade policies
and institutions, which undermines the profitability of their activities (Mzizi 2010).
Mazinjika (2009) discovered that most WCBTs had little knowledge of their countries'
customs regimes and their related protocol, and the few that knew them had little
motivation to use them to facilitate trading activities.

Research on WCBTs has identified lot of challenges and constraints they
encounter. The most common constraints include: inadequate public and private
transportation; multiple control posts; multiple and arbitrary taxation of goods;
insecurity and harassment; limited market information; communication costs; language
barriers; and, problem of exchange (Dejene 2001; Mzizi 2010; Njikam and Tchouassi
2010). Due to the lack of a formal exchange bureaux, most traders resort to informal
(black) market exchange where the premium is often high and volatile.

A report of a survey undertaken by UNIFEM among 2,000 WCBTs between
2007 and 2009 showed that a great majority of women traders stated that the
proceeds from trading was the main source of income for their families (Southern
African Trust 2008). Furthermore, WCBTs address vital issues of livelihoods such
as food and income security (Mzizi 2010). They contribute to food security, by
trading in food products from areas of surplus to areas of deficit (Dejene 2001).
Because women cross-border trading is carried out informally, measuring their
contributions to national and regional economic development is difficult (Dejene
2001).

Rational Choice Theory

The basic principles of rational theory are derived from neo-classical economics.
Based on a variety of different models according to Ritzer (1996), Freidman and
Hechter (1988) put together what they describe as a 'Sketal' model of rational
choice theory. The focus of rational choice theory is on actors. Actors are seen as
being purposive, or as having intentionality. That is, actors have ends or goals toward
which their actions are aimed. Actors also have preferences (values and utilities).
The main assumption of this theory is that any action by an individual is a purposive
behaviour, which will hold benefits for the actor in some ways. Rational Choice
Theory sees individuals' behaviour as motivated by their wants, needs and goals. It is
also says that individuals act with specific given constraints that are based on the
information they have about the conditions under which they are acting.

The relationship between individuals' wants and the constraints in achieving them
can be seen in the pure technical terms of relationship of a means to an end and
since it is not possible to achieve all their desires and goals they have to make
choices in their goals and the means of achieving them. Rational Choice Theory
holds that individuals usually anticipate the outcomes of alternative courses of action
and calculate that which will be best for them. Rational individuals are believed to
choose the alternative that is likely to grant them their goals at the minimal cost.

There are two types of decision-making identified by Rational Choice theorists, namely, involvement decisions and event decisions. Involvement decisions are those in which choices are made to become involved in an act or behaviour, and the continuity or retreat from such behaviour depends on the weight of costs and benefit of it, while event decisions are those in which the strategies of carrying out an action are determined. If these strategies are difficult, such course of action or behaviour will not be taken.

The argument of this research is anchored on the notion that economic activity of cross-border trading is rooted in rational choice theory as any individual, before opting for cross-border trading, will have to weigh the pros and cons of such decision. And since cross-border trading does not require much capital, it is an easy option for women as a means of easing economic repression. Along the line, as cross-border traders realize that the rewards/profits accrued from cross-border trade far outweigh its costs, they develop tactics to cope and minimize whatever costs and difficulties are associated with the trade. It goes a long way to explain why there has been a steady increase in women's involvement in ICBT in recent times; bringing to the fore the fact that an activity becomes attractive if its potential benefits outweigh the potential danger and cost associated with it. That adequately explains why women persist in ICBT despite the challenges and difficulties associated with the trade.

Method of Data Collection

The itinerary nature of informal trade militates against the availability of data concerning informal economic actors. Qualitative methods of data collection were therefore found appropriate for this type of work. The qualitative methods of data collection utilized in this study include: Unstructured Observations; Focus Group Discussions (FGDs); In-depth Interviewing (IDI); and; Key-Informant Interviewing (KII).

Unstructured observations were carried out at Seme Border, Iyana-Iba and Mile-Two motor parks. These motor parks are used to convey goods from Abidjan through Ghana, Togo and Benin Republic to various destinations in Nigeria. The essence of the unstructured observation was to get familiar with the operations of women traders coming from these West African countries.

Two focus group discussions (FGDs) were carried out at Iyana-Iba and Mile-Two motor parks. It was virtually impossible to conduct an FGD at Seme Border because of the visible fear of the uniformed personnel expressed by women traders. At Iyana-Iba and Mile Two motor parks, the focus group discussions were carried out with women traders as they waited for their goods to arrive or for a loading vehicle to fill up. The researcher and research assistants would go to the parks to wait for the women to arrive. However, the consent of women to participate in FGDs was sought through contact persons (drivers).

In all, 30 in-depth interviews were carried out at various times and different places. Sometimes, the researcher and research assistant had to follow the women in public vehicles to get them interviewed. The purpose of the interview was explained to them, to get their consent to be interviewed.

A total of 10 key informants were included in the study. The key informants include the custom officials, immigration and police officers and the drivers at the motor parks where the women board vehicles to various destinations.

Women involved in cross-border trade were interviewed for the period spanning eight months. The information was tape-recorded, transcribed, and analysed through content analysis and ethnographic summaries.

Results and Critical Discussions

Motivation and Social Networking Among Women Traders in Informal Cross-border Trade

Normally, a person will not start a business without motivation (Robertson 2003). Motivation is an important factor in the decision to start a business. There are various and possible factors that could influence women entrepreneurial behaviours despite the fact that culturally, women are expected to stay at home, take care of children, and play other social roles (Ehigie and Idemudia 2000). Women are the primary agents of socialization; it has been posited that the absence of mothers at home over a long period often leads to deviant behaviour among children (Olutayo 2005). Despite the culturally approved roles of women in society, the majority of the women were engaged in cross-border trading for economic survival reasons and to supplement the family income. One important motivation factor found in this study is the 'quick returns on investment and location opportunity'. Some of the women said they got involved in informal cross-border trading (ICBT) because of the proximity of the border (Seme Border) to their residence. The proximity enabled them to do quick trading and return home when they completed their business. Some of the respondents elaborated on this issue.

> There is no other means to support my husband, who had been retrenched from his place of work. ICBT brings in quick money and it has helped us to live above poverty level in my household (Female / 35 years/ IDI/ February 2012).

> There is no other way to generate income to train my children and support my husband. I will continue to remain a cross-border trader because it generates quick money. Since there is no other means to get money to feed, the only means I know is what I will stick to (FGD Respondent/ 40 years/ April 2012)

> I live not far from Seme Border. Most times, I travelled to Cotonou to purchase some goods for sale at the office. I added ICBT to my job because my salary is not sufficient to meet my financial burdens. I will continue as a cross border trader until my financial burden decreases (IDI/ 38 years/ April 2012).

The location advantage was corroborated by the customs personnel. A key informant said that there were usually intermarriage between Nigerians and Beninois and some of them lived around the border town. The dual citizenship gave them advantage in crossing from one country to the other. This had been one of the obstacles preventing immigration officials from enforcing the law, as people always claimed they were in their countries. Findings also revealed the social networks the traders were involved in. The majority of women traders were introduced to the business by friends and relatives. These friends and relatives taught them the rules of the game, that is, how to cope and succeed in spite of the difficulties associated with the trade.

Trading Activities Across ECOWAS Sub-region Borders – Known and Unknown Risks

Women in informal cross-border trade engage in the sale of different and diverse commodities which are categorized differently. There are agricultural products like rice, pastry, cooking oil, beef, chicken and different kinds of fruits. The other category is textile materials which include Ankara, Guinea Brocade, Lace, among others, and old second-hand materials called *okirika*. *Okirika* includes different types of wear, shoes, bags and bed spreads. All these items are categorized as banned goods.

Findings reveal that women in informal cross-border trading had to travel to markets in Benin Republic to buy all these commodities. Some went as far as other countries like Ghana, Togo and Cote d'Ivoire to purchase some commodities if such commodities were not available in Benin Republic. However, women in informal cross-border trade across the sub-ECOWAS region did not use available formal systems and structures for their transactions, which exposed them to known and unknown risks along the region. In addition, their mode of operations made it difficult for regional trade policy initiatives to have any significant impact on their business. Two key informants were apt on this:

> There are policies that guide international trade that, anyone who engages in it must adhere to. The status of women had been raised from an ordinary woman to international trader immediately she makes a decision to leave her country and cross to another country to trade. However, most of the women in informal trade are not knowledgeable about the law that guides international trading. They do not know how to be a cross border trader. Most of them are not registered to take full advantages of ECOWAS Liberalized policy (KII/59 years/March 2012).

> All kinds of women on daily basis ply Lagos-Seme Border en-route to other towns in Nigeria. It is observed for several years that cross-border traders do not have legal documents needed to facilitate such trade. Most of them do not have ECOWAS passport and international identity. Majority of the women in cross-border trade are illiterate, but have business initiatives and are so desperate while engaging in the business. The literate ones among them are very few (KII/55 years/ March 2012).

Ironically, findings revealed that women traders showed little knowledge about policies guiding cross-border trading except the fact that they had to carry an international passport when crossing the border which most of them claimed they did not possess. The few of them that possessed the international passport believed that they would be delayed at transit points, and would be asked to pay a fee of two thousand naira before they can enter. Most of the women showed little motivation to register and pay the little tax required on their goods. Likewise, they were not aware that they could purchase goods with a minimum of $500 if they were registered, without going through the bush-paths, or their goods being seized. The traders largely wanted to continue with the old way of trading they had practised for many decades. The preference for the old ways of trading was evident in the manner women traders were operating along ECOWAS sub-region borders.

Women traders gave several reasons for the lack of confidence that registration would assist them in cross-border trading. Women advanced cultural reasons such as the fact that they were women who were taking initiatives to train and cater for their children, and assist in the economies of their households. In so doing, they were helping themselves, families, their communities, and society in general. The general perception of women cross-border traders is that they are contributing significantly towards the development of nations, through provision of scarce items; therefore they should not be hindered in their bid to conduct successful businesses. Moreover, some of the women believed that they were small-scale traders that operated with small capital ranging from thirty thousand naira to hundred thousand naira. Women traders also looked at the issue of time and believed that they needed to conduct their businesses quickly in order to return home to take care of their children and spouses. Going through the formal process of registration would cut into the time they needed to conduct their businesses and return home.

A key informant corroborated this:

> When an immigration officer on guard prevents some of these women traders from entering the border, they are always ready to beg and plead with us, appealing that they had to take care of their families. While we allow the policy regulations to override the sentiments expressed by these women, some of them find their ways through the bush paths with the assistance of (Beninois). However, I believe that women traders should show themselves to immigration officer and registered because of their safety and inherent danger associated with travelling to another country (KII/ 45 years/ June 2012).

In addition, women traders also expressed the fear of tax payment as one reason they were not motivated to register. They believed that they might be unable to afford to pay the taxes, since they operated at the small-scale level. Payment of taxes would eat deep into their profits. They also expressed doubt that the tax the custom personnel would ask them to pay would appropriate. To the women respondents, custom officials were not sincere, as they would always find faults, with the hope of extorting more money than the exact amount they would be required to pay if they truly register as international traders. A woman respondent in an FGD expressed her fear thus:

> I doubt if official rate of taxation will be applied. We all knew from experience that customs, immigration, and other security men will always find reasons to demand more money in their individual capacities (FGD Participant/ 47 years/ May 2012).

Generally, women cross-border traders did not have good opinions about the uniformed personnel. They were of the opinion that any policy that would hinder customs, immigration and security officials from receiving bribes from women traders was bound to fail because the officials would not allow it to operate smoothly.

Challenges of Women in Informal Cross-border Trade

Several challenges have been associated with cross-border trading, more so with the informality associated with women traders' work. Obstacles do not necessarily stem from policy regulation, but from the informality of women's work. Several obstacles expressed by women traders ranged from attitude of uniformed personnel, to language barriers, sexual harassment, fluctuating exchange rate, vulnerability to HIV/AIDs and inadequate transport facilities. The obstacle that the women traders perceived as the most serious challenge they faced was the attitude of uniformed personnel. Their responses were not surprising, considering the fact that the work of uniformed personnel is based on formal procedure of operations which aim at checking the informality of women traders' activities.

Women in cross-border trading are perceived as smugglers (*fayawo*). Smuggling of banned goods into a country is seen as detrimental to national productivity and economic growth. the informality of the women's work in cross-border trading undermines the collection of the necessary revenues for the government purse. It is posited therefore that women in informal cross-border trading are perceived as 'enemies of nations'. This perception causes constant acrimony between uniformed personnel and women in informal cross- border trading. In one of the unstructured observation at a customs' checkpoint, the researcher witnessed a scuffle between a customs officer and a woman trader which resulted in the customs officer physically assaulting the woman trader.

One of the women respondents said:

> 'Custom is the main challenge WCBT encountered, and some women have had hypertension because of custom officials' attitudes of seizing their goods. Police, immigration officers are also part of the challenges of WCBT. Due to desperations by police and customs officers to get money, even when a vehicle is not carrying any contraband goods, they will still attempt to seize goods and demand for money before they can return the goods or detain the vehicle until he pays them' (FGD/38 years/ May 2012).

Theft, Robbery of Goods and Fraud in the Market

The findings show that the majority of the women were particular about the cases of robbery and theft carried out by hooligans and sometimes by drivers under the guise of helping the women load their goods. The women respondents identified this problem as being related to the insecurity at the border. Unstructured observation at the border revealed that it was porous. People from various ethnic backgrounds were within the border town engaging in one business or the other. More so, there were no officials on patrol to check their activities.

Another observation made at the Seme border showed that many of the WCBTs were not usually at peace until *crossers* (people helping transport goods from another country) or truck men brought their goods; and even after that, they monitored the drivers of the buses they were boarding like a *'mother hen'* until the vehicle started off. Observation revealed that hooligans/touts (*agbero*) always charged women traders some amount known as *'land money'* on their goods. Scuffles usually ensued which sometimes resulted in the goods being stolen if the women traders refused to pay land charges to *'agbero'*. The logic behind this was the perception that women in informal cross-border trading were engaging in illegal business and, therefore, they had no choice but to obey the hooligans. It was reasoned that hooligans did not tamper with women in formal cross-border trade. In this regard, therefore, money paid to hooligans could have been used for taxes if women in informal cross-border trading had been properly registered. The problem of theft and robbery by drivers and hooligans, together with fraud, is illuminated by the response of a woman in focus group discussion thus:

> There are many people at this border. Many of them are theft [sic] waiting to steal the goods of anyone who is not watchful. If one is not watchful, the hooligans at the garage will steal one's goods. Again, the *'agbero'* will come and charge *owo-ile* (Land Charges) as if the land belongs to them. Moreover, if one refuses to pay, they will start dragging your goods with you. They even prefer to steal your goods than collecting *owo-ile* (Land Charges) from you. One needs to be very smart in this border (FGD Participant/ 47 yrs/ April 2012)

None of the women respondents claimed to have contacted HIV/AIDS. With regard to sexual harassment by the uniformed personnel, there was unanimous opinion that customs personnel usually harassed women sexually. However, no one among the respondents claimed to have been harassed before by customs personnel. Their position was understandable, considering that in Yoruba culture or any other culture in Nigeria, women cannot come out boldly to admit that they have been harassed sexually because of the stigmatization involved. Ironically, there was a sort of subtle acknowledgement and emotional understanding among the women traders that, sometimes, a woman might give in to the sexual demands of the customs men in order to prevent seizure of her goods. The more serious question for a woman to ponder was: If she lost her goods through seizure, how would she cope and take care of her family?

However, a key informant explained the situation on sexual harassment in another dimension

> Harassment occurs at most routes of the border, both legal and illegal routes. Border officials spearheaded some, while women traders themselves engineered some. The women who ply these illegal routes while transacting business are at the mercy of themselves when caught by patrol officers on duty. However, 90% of harassments that occurred at the border areas were usually fashioned by these women. Since

women traders traded in contraband goods, when they are caught and the goods are seized, they would chose to entice border officials on duty as a means to liberate their goods. They are ready to give anything' (KII/55 years/ May 2012).

Another challenge that was worth noting was the health challenge associated with cross-border trading. The main health challenge expressed by the women respondents was stress. The majority of women traders experienced stress in the course of travelling to another country for several reasons. One reason was the fear of seizure of goods by customs officials. The other reason concerned their fear of thefts by drivers or touts at the motor parks, and extortion by different uniformed men. A woman respondent explained thus:

> Though, the gain of CBT is high, it is too stressful because of the challenges we normally experience on this route. However, if God has not opened another one, I will continue with this. The problem and stress associated with this trade tells on one's health; it is not a trade one should do for a long time, if one wants to enjoy. The problem of CBT at Seme border is much; if you see my picture, you will realize that the stress of CBT is not good for the health (IDI/ 39 years/June 2012).

Despite the apparent challenges involved in cross-border trade, the majority of the respondents said they would remain cross-border traders, because they had no other means of income to train their children. It is pertinent to point out that because of insistence of women to continue with informal cross-border trading, the majority of them had devised several coping strategies to negotiate these challenges.

Coping Strategies of Women Traders in Informal Cross-border Trade in the ECOWAS Sub-region

A coping strategy is an important effort or plan devised by a person or a group to achieve any laudable objectives (Lazaru 1986). Women in informal cross-border trade devised various coping strategies to negotiate challenges associated with the informality of their type of trading. Among the notable ones is what is known as 'Settling Drivers'. The drivers conveying the goods act as intermediaries between the women traders and customs officials. The findings revealed that drivers conveying goods for women traders usually charged women with merchandise higher amount than those without such goods. For instance, before the removal of the fuel subsidy, bus fare from Seme border to Iyana-Iba cost two hundred naira for people without merchandise, while those with merchandise paid as much as two to three thousand naira depending on the quantity of goods. The extra amounts were used to settle the requirements of the uniformed personnel. The majority of the women preferred this method to dealing with customs officials themselves.

A respondent said:

> If you have paid the driver sufficiently, the driver will settle the officers, so once I pay; the customs are no longer my problems (IDI/35 years/ February 2012).

The findings also revealed that in a situation where customs officers demanded for money higher than what women had contributed, women traders would contribute more money among themselves to 'settle' such officers. It is important to mention that the majority of women traders preferred this method to dealing with customs officials individually. Women traders also differentiated between 'seized' and 'seizure'. When one's goods were 'seized', there was still hope of recovering such goods; but when they entered 'seizure', they could not be recovered. Thus, most women bribed customs officials in other to avoid their goods entering 'seizure', and money contributed was usually accompanied with lots of pleas.

The findings revealed that women traders were sometimes charged a particular amount to bail their goods when seized. A respondent said:

> Customs have specific period for specific goods, for examples, if it is the era of rice seizure, one will be billed two thousand naira for a bag of rice and one thousand five hundred to bail a cartoon of turkey. This implies that the number of bags of rice or cartoons of turkey one can afford to bail is what one takes home; as such, it will affect the profit margin. The moment we bail out goods, such trip will yield no profit, for all the profits have been given out to custom to bail out the goods (IDI/ 32 years/ January 2012).

However, some women went to the market every day to buy in small quantities, the rationale behind this being to avoid seizure by customs officials. Some women also divided goods into different portions due to fear that if they carried their goods in one vehicle, customs officials were likely to seize them. They calculated that if the goods were divided into different portions and transported in different vehicles, it was not likely that all the goods would be seized.

Summary and Conclusion

Informal cross-border trade (ICBT) is a vital part of the regional economy that cannot be ignored. ICBT has provided jobs for a significant number of people, particularly women. It has provided easy entry for the unemployed and the retrenched. It has helped many people, especially women, to train their children, support their spouses and provide for household economy. It has enabled women to live and rise above the poverty level. The findings from this study show that the majority of women are into this trade because it offers quick returns which have enabled them to supplement family income, train children and support their spouses. The proximity of the border town to some of the women's residences has also been seen as added advantage.

However, despite the significant advantages that informal cross-border trading has provided for women in particular, there is much government and non-governmental organizations need to do to educate women on the inherent dangers associated with informality of their trading activities. Of importance to this issue are the known risks associated with informality. Cross-border trade involves a high level of insecurity related to both persons and goods engendered by corrupt law-enforcement agencies and touts. Traders carrying money run the risk of having it seized. This study corroborated the findings by Ibeanu (2007) that one in two respondents had experienced some form of harassment during their trip. The Nigeria-

Benin border is considered particularly problematic, and has defied solutions in spite of joint border patrols organized at the behest of the two countries' presidents. The insecurity experienced by women traders is compounded by the fact that they often do not have valid travel documents and do not always know whether they need to pay taxes on the goods they carry.

Many women traders have devised strategies to cross borders with their goods. The situation at the borders fuels extortion. Not surprisingly, those interviewed mentioned extortion by law enforcement officials as the problem they encountered most frequently. It is also important to underline the fact that the majority of women reported that their businesses had been adversely affected. It has also been shown through respondents' contributions that travelling outside one's country is fraught with many unknown risks. If such travelling happens without the knowledge of immigration officers, the government of that country would be unable to offer any diplomatic support.

Recommendations

1. There is need to address the issue of informality in mainstream trade policy making and to strengthen the notion that women informal traders are also important clients of the ministries of trade and regional economic communities. Every effort should be made to enable women traders build trust in formal cross-border trading structures rather than continuing with the old practices of informal trading. Apart from the fact that illegality poses unpredictable costs that make planning difficult, it prevents women traders from securing recognition from formal government structures, which leaves their contributions unrecorded and therefore not recognized.

2. More research should be conducted to document the experiences of women traders at all border points and within their business premises. While it is important to find ways of quantifying their participation, it would be better from a strategic viewpoint to use qualitative methods to assess their experiences and learn from them the constraints that hamper regional trade.

3. The use of the mass media to disseminate information concerning trade policy on the sub-ECOWAS region should be encouraged. National governments, regional bodies and most civil society organizations should educate or empower the women with knowledge on how they can participate formally and more meaningfully in regional trade. Often, these women rely on each other for socio-economic support and accessing information, all of which they do in very informal settings.

4. Policy implementation should include production and dissemination of innovative knowledge products to: (i) ensure visibility of the contributions of women cross-border traders to wealth creation, poverty reduction, employment creation, and regional integration; (ii) disseminate best practices in supporting women informal cross-border traders; and (iii) fight stigmatization of and violence against women informal cross-border traders.

References

Ackello-Ogutu, C., 1997, 'Unrecorded cross-border trade between Kenya and Uganda: Implications for food security', SD Publication Series, Office of Sustainable Development Bureau for Africa, USAID, Technical Paper 59, July.

Cagatay, N. and Ozler, S., 1995, 'Feminization of the labour Force: the effects of long term Development and structural Adjustment', *World Development* 23 (11): 1883-1894.

Chichilinsky, G., 2003, 'Globalization and Cross Border Exchange', Available at www. Amalik.iijournals.com, Accessed March 2012.

Dejene, V., 2001, 'Women's Cross-Border Trade in West-Africa', Available at www. Widetech.Org, Accessed February 2012.

Desai, M., 2009, 'Women Cross Border Traders Rethinking global trade', Available at www. Pelgrave Journlas.com, Accessed February 2012.

Economic Commission for Africa, 2010, 'Gender and Intra Africa trade: The Case of west-Africa', Available at www. UNESCA. Org, Accessed March 2012.

ECOWAS-WAEMU, 2006, 'Regional integration for growth and poverty reduction in West Africa: Strategies and plan of action', Regional strategy paper prepared by the WAEMU Commission and the ECOWAS Executive Secretariat, Abuja and Ouagadougou, December.

Ehigie, B.O., Idemudia, V.O., 2000, 'Working women and exclusive breast-feeding in Oyo State, Nigeria', *African Journal of Business and Economic Research*, 1(1): 49-57.

Goldberg, P.K., Pavenik, N.L., 2003, 'The Response of the Informal Sector to Trade Liberalization', *Journal of Developmental Economics*, 72: 463-496.

Ibeanu, O., 2007, 'Beyond declarations: Law enforcement officials and ECOWAS protocols free movement of persons and goods in West Africa', CLEEN Foundation, Available at www.Cleen.Org, Accessed March 2012.

IOM Southern Africa Newsletter, 2010, 'Informal Cross Border Trade. Eye Issue on migration Health', Available at www. iomzimbabwe. org, Accessed March 2012.

Kabira, W.M., 2006, 'Women and cross Border Trade in East Africa', Available at www.library .fes.de, Accessed March 2012.

Lazarus, R.S., 1986, 'An analysis of Coping in Middle-Aged Community', *Journal of Personality and Social Psychology*, 50: 992-1003.

Matsuyama, R., 2011, 'Risky business of informal cross border trade' Available at www. Afronews.com, Accessed April 2012.

Masinjika, M., 2009, 'Gender Dimensions of Cross-Border Trade in East Africa Communities', Available at http://www.uneca.org, Accessed May 2012.

Mijere, N.J., 2006, 'Informal Cross-border Trade in the South African Development', Available at www. Ossrea.com, Accessed April 2012.

Mzizi, L., 2010, 'The Nature of Informal Cross Border Trade', Available at www.Times.co.sz, Accessed May 2012.

Morris, G. and Saul, M., 2000, 'Women's Business links; A preliminary Assessment of Women Cross border Traders', Available at www. Pdf.usaid .gov, Accessed April 2012.

Muzvidiziwa, V., 1998, 'Cross Border Trade: A strategy for climbing out of Poverty', Available at www. Digital. lib.msu.edu, Accessed April 2012.

Njikam, O. and Tchouassi, G., 2010, 'Women in informal cross-border trade: Evidence from the Central African Region', *Academic Journals*, 6 (5): 22-31.

Olutayo, O., 2005, 'Women in Informal Long-Distance Trade: The Family and Rural-Urban Market Nexus in Southwestern Nigeria', *Ibadan Journal of the Social Sciences*, 3(2):67

Ritzer, G., 1999, *Sociological Theory*, Fourth Edition, McGraw Hill International Editions, Sociology Series.

Robinson, S., 2003, 'An examination of entrepreneurial motives and their influence on the way rural women small business owners manage their employees', *Journal of Developmental Entrepreneurship*, 6(2): 151-167.

Shamu, S., 2005, 'Gender and Entrepreneurship: Survival Strategies of Tanzania-bound Zimbabwean Informal Women Cross Border Traders', Available at http://www.ossrea.net, Retrieved April 2012.

Southern African Trust, 2008, 'Unleashing the Potential of Women Cross Border Traders', Available at http://www.unwomen.org, Retrieved November 2011.

Tsikata, D., 2009, 'Informalization, the informal economy and urban women's livelihoods in sub-Saharan Africa since the 1990s', in S. Razavi, ed., *The Gendered Impacts of Liberation: Towards 'Embedded Liberalism?'* New York, Routledge.

UNIFEM, 2008, 'Unleashing the Potential of Women in Informal Cross Border Traders to Transform Intra-African Trade', Available at www.UNIFEM.org, Accessed May 2012.

6

Regional Networking and Identity Integration in West Africa: Case Study of Ejigbo-Yoruba in Cote d'Ivoire

Adebusuyi I. Adeniran and Akinpelu O. Olutayo

Introduction

Essentially, cross-border network process predicated upon ethnic identity is seen as being stimulated by a relatively high level of risk aversion; bounded by moral and behavioural prescripts from the 'home front'. Meanwhile, varying reasons could generally be adduced as the motives for people engaging in cross-border interaction. Some have been insistent on having a feel or an experience of other societies; as such 'dropping out of the continuity of life'. While such individuals have existed across human histories, they have been observed as an insignificant component whose impact cannot account for such huge movement of people across national territories (Kivisto and Faist 2010:1). Instead, prevalent developments within the immediate social world have been the main motivating propensities; that is, the 'push factors', for instance, the desire to enhance individuals' standard of living (economic cause); to avoid social turmoil/political repression (political cause); to escape natural disaster (environmental cause) and sometimes to facilitate religious expression (spiritual cause).

On the other hand, when factors drawing people into another society are more active than those discouraging them, they tend to move. Such 'pull factors' have included better conditions of living, security of life and property, sustainable access to social resources, job opportunities and relative higher wages. The relevant intensity of these factors contributes to the 'volume' and defines the specific nature of the 'stream', moving from point A to point B, instead of point C (Lee 1966:50). Routinely, when people move, they embark on a journey of hope and uncertainty whether within or across international borders.

Trans-border movements, for purposes of trade and/or work, have become the most widespread pattern, especially since the colonial and immediate post-colonial era, in parts of West Africa. For several decades, such migrants' networks, as the Ejigbo-Yoruba have contributed in no little measure to the emergence of a series of market centres in West Africa (Asiwaju 1992). Unusually, businesses are transacted without much regard for international boundaries. Of course, related long-established, pre-colonial mode of interaction has outwitted the contemporary national demarcation in such cases. For instance, the situation with the Ejigbo-Yoruba from former 'British Nigeria', who have found it easier to trade and settle in a former 'French colonial state' like Cote d'Ivoire overlooking extant; impeding tendencies, is a good case at hand. Indeed, this case has become more significant and interesting in the light of the ongoing intent of the ECOWAS to transform the regional body from 'an ECOWAS of States to an ECOWAS of People'. This is basically envisaged as an enabling platform for guaranteeing 'free movement of persons and goods' within the sub-region; thereby, giving imperative lifeline to the regional integrative-cum-developmental proposition (ECOWAS 2010). Besides facilitating the process of socio-economic unification of the ECOWAS sub-region, ongoing cross-border activities of the Ejigbo-Yoruba along the Nigerian-Ivorian migratory corridor has been oiling the process of inter-community development in West Africa. As they are contributing to the development process of the host society, so also Ejigbo-Yoruba are engaging in the socio-economic transformation of their point of departure in Nigeria.

Objectives of Study

The following objectives drive the study:
  i.   To explore relevant socio-historical underpinnings driving contemporary cross-border interaction in West Africa;
  ii. To examine the sustainability of prevalent cross-border networking system in West Africa;
  iii. To explain the outcomes of identity interposition, along the Nigerian-Ivorian migratory corridor, for the process of regional integration in West Africa; and;
  iv. To establish a relationship between identity integration and regional development in West Africa.

Study's Methodology

Being essentially a reflexive exploratory study, relevant qualitative data collection techniques (non-participant observation, in-depth interviews [IDIs], focus group discussions [FGDs] and case study) were utilized in generating primary data for the study from the two study locations of Ejigbo, Nigeria and Abidjan, Cote d'Ivoire. This was done in order to provide the study with useful first-hand information on the nature of cross-border networking and mode of constructing 'self' within the transnational social space. Content analysis and ethnographic summaries were engaged in the process of data coding and analysis.

In Abidjan, only Ejigbo-Yoruba immigrants who have stayed for a minimum of five years in Cote d'Ivoire were engaged in the study, and in Ejigbo, only Ejigbo-Yoruba returnees of a minimum of five years stay in Nigeria were involved in the study. A pilot study preceded each of the main surveys in the two study locations in order to pre-test the potentiality of the research instruments and, indeed, to get accustomed to the study's locations.

Historical Constructs of Social Network and Migration System in West Africa

Drawing from the submissions of earlier social network scholars, Tilly (1996), among other new age network analysts, had presented a contextual positioning of social network as a sociological paradigm, especially as it pertains to migrants and the migration process. Core to his network summation is the assertion that history serves as a critical component in analysing social change, especially within the transnational realm. According to Tilly, all investigating sociologists of social life formation (such as is obtainable in the migratory process) and social structure should view social processes and social structures as being, first, historically contingent. In this way, the pattern and nature of migration to other locales could only be interpreted in relation to the connotation of such evolving social networks.

However, contrary to the logics of minimizing distances and multiplying opportunities, over and over again, individuals have sought to establish regular migration between two widely separated locations, and then concentrated their migration within such bipolar system rather than continuing their search for opportunities outside of it. The long chain, history of exchange between such bipolar migratory points has made the contemporary movement flourishing. Chain migration in this regard is, of course, the arrangements in which social ties persist between people of a particular origin of migration and people of a particular destination of migration, with people at the destination sending back information about new opportunities, recruiting new migrants and helping them to make the move. This form of cross-border interaction has been noted in the nature of prevalent migration pattern among the Ejigbo-Yoruba in Cote d'Ivoire. Despite prevalent colonial, cultural and geographical impediments between Nigeria and Cote d'Ivoire, the Ejigbo-Yoruba have been able to sustain the long established chain of migration over the years — that is, between Nigeria and Cote d'Ivoire; though a 'supposed' sister nation of Ghana, and two other West African countries – Togo and Republic of Benin – have to be crossed (see Figure 1 below).

Figuere 1: Map of West Africa showing the migratory poles and the transit points

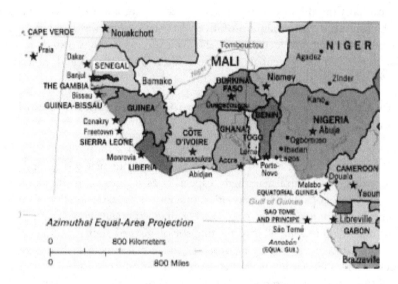

Source: http://un.org/Depts/Cartographic/map/profile/westafrica.pdf, accessed 06/08/2011

Contextually, the nature of cross-border networking and migration processes within the West African sub-region could be situated across three epochs; that is, pre-colonial, colonial and post-colonial eras. Meanwhile, a pre-colonial classification of related practices as intra-border or cross-border could be essentially infeasible for obvious situational exigencies. The first of such difficulties is the fact that the region could not be distinctively identified as a group of independent nations as at then (Alkali 1985). Numerous ethnic nationalities existed in kingdoms and empires within the geographical space of contemporary West Africa. Nevertheless, the existence of cross-border interaction was evident in the movement of indigenes who either participated in slave trading and inter-tribal wars or who were all together victims. Equally, trading activities across the Sahara and nomadic herding has caused human mobility and migration across parts of Africa. The dynamics of free movement of persons, inside and outside of empires and kingdoms of West African communities, were facilitated by the lack of such ostensibly defined border lines between and among the hitherto existing human settlements.. It is worth noting that, while most of the ethnic groups that left the old Borno Empire now occupy parts of various northern Francophone countries, most of the ethnic groups that left the defunct Oyo Empire, especially the Yoruba, are presently spread across parts of both Francophone and Anglophone countries neighbouring contemporary Nigeria (Akinjogbin 1980; Mahadi 1989). Indeed, the fall of the old Oyo Empire as a result of the nineteenth century invasion of parts of Yorubaland by the Fulani jihadists had facilitated the dispersions of the Yoruba to other West African states, the establishment of various migrants' settlements and the emergence of booming commercial activities at such locations. This has been enabled by the vastness of the old Oyo Empire (see Figure 2 below), which extended to the west, to areas of Ashanti, Dahomey and as far as present-day Togo (Akinjogbin 1980).

Figure 2: Map of Nigeria showing the limits of old Oyo Empire

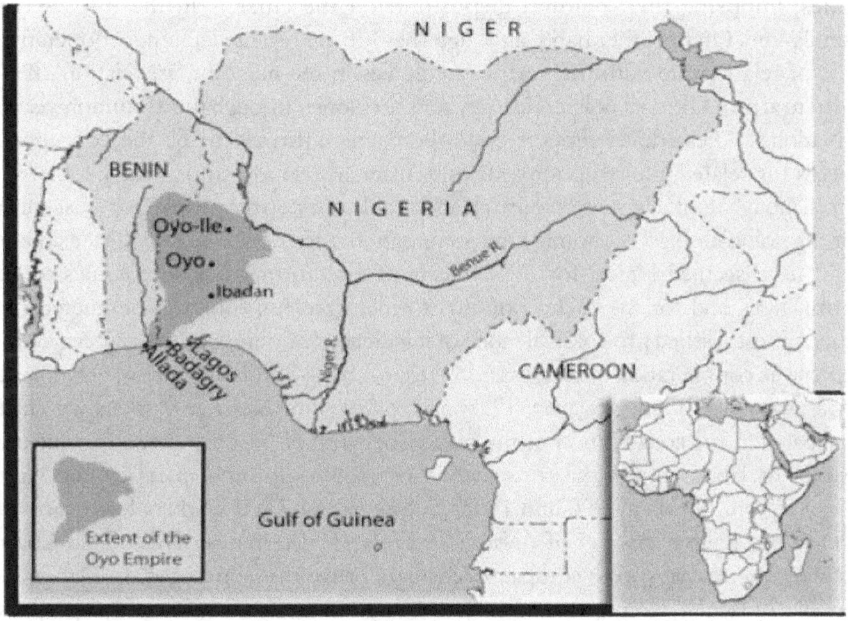

Source: http://brown.edu/Faculties/Haffenreffer/yoruba2.html, accessed on 06/08/2011

Accordingly, the Yoruba have come in contact with individuals from such West African countries as the Republics of Ghana, Benin, Togo, Cote d'Ivoire and Liberia. While the Ogbomoso-Yoruba are mainly found in parts of present-day Ghana, the Ejigbo-Yoruba are predominant in present-day Cote d'Ivoire, especially in Abidjan (Afolayan 2004; Lawan 2004). At another realm, the capture and trade of slaves in many parts of present-day Nigeria, including the Yoruba areas, which began around 1500, did result in forced displacement of populations. Impliedly, the trans-border migration of the Yoruba including the Ejigbo-Yoruba to locations considered safer for them, especially within the West African sub-region, had been necessitated. Also, *l'océan vers des terres* the search for arms and ammunition for the prosecution of prevalent inter-ethnic wars of the nineteenth century by traders of Yoruba ethnic descent did facilitate imperative contact and eventual settlement of some of them in such neighbouring Anglophone and Francophone countries, conspicuously before the advent of colonial rule (Adeniran 2009:3676-8).

Des études portant sur la migration interne de la main-d'œuvre ont aussi révélé que, Although colonial economic policies within the emergent West African nation-states promoted an export-based economy and movement from various hinterlands to the emerging urban settlements, they indirectly discouraged cross-border interactions, especially along the Anglophone/Francophone dichotomy. Such dichotomy was to play a significant role in the formation of national outlooks for such emergent political entities in West Africa, for instance. On the one hand, the French took over some of the political entities, imposing their cultural disposition on the citizens in the disguise of 'assimilation'. On the other hand, although the British presented a rather cooperative mode of relationship with their African colonies in the name of 'association', they tended to affirm a distinct political identity for the colonies through the 'Commonwealth of Nations'. These developments could be readily affirmed to be the conceptual impetus for related, contemporary identity misinterpretation among the people.

Yet, though ironically, such colonial creation could not stop the people from sustaining their pre-colonial socio-economic interactive patterns after colonial rule. Ostensibly, it would have seemed logical for the subjects of two former British colonies to be intermingling, and for the citizens of two former French colonies to be interacting. Rather, the established pre-colonial mode of interaction has outwitted the contemporary nationalistic configuration in such cases. As regards trans-border migration within West Africa, Abba (1993) and Afolayan (1998) affirm that some Nigerian workers who had participated in the construction of the railway network of Nigeria, were subsequently recruited as labourers for the construction of railways in other parts of the West African region. Between 1900 and 1902, an estimate of 7,000 workers left Lagos to work on the Railway project of *Sekondi-Tarkwa* and gold mines of the Gold Coast (Ghana), where wages were comparatively higher than those in Lagos. In Dahomey (Republic of Benin), many Nigerian emigrants began to trade after the railway projects were completed, and many others were to head for Cote d'Ivoire after the World War I. Many emigrants from Nigeria were apparently attracted by the conviction that it was easier to eke out a living across the border, and, over time, the wives and wards joined their husbands (Adegbola 1972), thus oiling the chain of existing cross-border networking across the West African sub-region.

Cross-border Interaction and Migration in West Africa

Over time, related ethnic affiliation of the people has tended to determine the patterns and structure of the migratory network obtainable within the West African sub-region. That is, individuals' subsisting interpersonal social ties do serve as measurements of prevalent social capital amidst them. The ensuing interaction, and subsequent movement have been taking a direct negotiating path since all obtainable social capital at the level of familial and communal interactions are usually pleaded within the network functioning. According to an Ejigbo-Yoruba migrant in Abidjan:

> .....in our family, the first person that came to Cote d'Ivoire was my paternal uncle...who invited his younger brother...that later brought me upon attainment of 'freedom' (IDI, Male, Vulcanizer, 40 years, Abidjan, 19 June 2010).

Alternatively, when a 'would be' migrant decides to network himself or herself without utilizing such available familial and communal affiliations, then the entailed process becomes an 'indirect one'. Varying networks of unfamiliar individuals ('crossers') would become essential at various border posts, and along the migratory route until such migrants get to the point of destination where the ethnic network could then be useful. Generally, the need for more reliable helping hands in Cote d'Ivoire as a result of business expansion, has been encouraging the recruitment of wards of immediate family members from the home front in comparison with other sources. An Ejigbo-Yoruba female business owner in Abidjan surmises:

> ......this explains why the continued growth of the network pattern has been predicated largely upon familial attachment (FGD, Female, 40 years+, Abidjan, 26 June 2010; Observations, Abidjan, 22–30 June 2010).

It is, however, common knowledge within the migrants' network that it is much more profitable and prestigious to facilitate the relocation of relatives from home (that is, Nigeria), who will work for them than taking up Ivorian or foreign workers. One, aside from the transport fare from Ejigbo (Nigeria) to Abidjan (Cote d'Ivoire), no remuneration is usually attached for work done after arrival. Two, for facilitating such trips for relatives, an immeasurable degree of honour and regards is routinely adduced by family members to the migrants who provided the platform for others to utilize. Three, the social base of affected facilitators is usually enhanced within the Ivorian social space, since 'number' is paramount in the interaction of various migrants' communities with the host society (the state in particular), especially when it comes to politicking. A female case profile states:

> .....I have lost count of those who have made it to Abidjan through me....it is also to my advantage to bring them.... (Case Profile 1, Female, Shop Owner, 52 years, Adjame-Abidjan, 20 June 2010).

With the number of apprentices in her shops, ostensibly recruited from 'home', there is no doubt the fact that it is to her 'advantage' to bring them (the migrants). Meanwhile, it is obvious that established network members as the 'case study' above have not been the sole beneficiaries of the network process; also, the 'recruited apprentices' and the family members left behind in Ejigbo, Nigeria do benefit from the entire process. While the apprentices are assisted to set up their own businesses when the time to obtain 'freedom' matures, intermittently, goods and funds are sent to relatives left behind courtesy of the service being rendered by the apprentices. The texts of the following IDIs seem to be in appropriate consonance:

> .....my sister paid for my trip to Abidjan....I lived with her and served in her shop before she helped me to set up my own shop (IDI, Female, Provision Seller, 33 years, Adjame-Abidjan, 27 June 2010)

> ....from what I have been telling you....you would see that there is no way I could have made it here without my relations, especially my uncle who actually paid for my transport fare from home (Ejigbo, Nigeria) (IDI, Male, Nursery Teacher, 34 years, Semisel-Abidjan, 28 June 2010).

Generally, the process of the 'apprentices' obtaining 'freedom' from their 'masters' and 'mistresses' entail rendering of unspecified and unremunerated services within a given period of time. Thereafter, such 'apprentices' are provided with funds, equipment and shops to begin their own life. At this point such 'apprentices' are relieved of all forms of control and supervision from their 'masters' and 'mistresses' (Observations, Abidjan, 20 June 2010).

Nevertheless, it has been very glaring that prevalent interpersonal ties, and sometimes, communal ties, have been the precursors of prevalent familial patterns of the migration network of the Ejigbo-Yoruba along the Nigerian-Ivorian corridor over the years.

Interposition of Nigerian and Ivorian Identity Within the Transnational Social Space

Ostensibly, the socio-economic environment in Cote d'Ivoire has made it expedient for the Ejigbo-Yoruba migrants to identify with the Ivorian community. One of the most visible ways, however, is through language and dressing; though oftentimes for merely business and survival sake:

> ....environment matters....because among those who made Cote d'Ivoire great we have Nigerians; also among those who made it bad, we have Nigerians..... in the market I speak French and dress like the Ivorian; amidst Nigerians, I behave normally... (IDI, Female, 35 years, Trader, Semisel-Abidjan, 22 June 2010).

The 'environment' from the above submission is indicative of the deterministic tendency of the social space in the process of identity projection. On the other hand, the 'normal behaviour' points to the engagement of disposition that is basically Nigerian within household interactions, and amidst fellow migrants, unlike interactions within larger Ivorian social space. Essentially, the migrants' network, which has the 'Oba' as its central symbol, usually plays a prominent role in fashioning out a tenable identity (identities) for individual Ejigbo-Yoruba migrants within the Ivorian social space. Such identity construction was routinely carried out with the economic goals of the affected migrants kept in focus. Preceding potent integration into the Ivorian society, the need for language re-orientation is crucial as noted earlier. Of all the languages, the colloquial Abidjan French is mandatory. Respective migrants' relatives, tribal friends and neighbours often perform a significant role in this respect. As soon as one is able to speak an indigenous language, the Ivorian permanent residence permit (*card identete*) is normally processed through the 'Oba'. The 'Oba' performs an intermediary role between the government and his subjects. He is deemed to be the custodian of the migrants who fall within his jurisdiction; the Ejigbo-Yoruba migrants in this case. Interestingly, this is the pattern routinely employed by the Ivorian authorities in relating to other migrant network groups from other West African countries.

> The *'card identete'* is compulsory for all foreigners; without it you cannot get anything in Cote d'Ivoire. In hospitals, schools and during election you will need the *'card identete'* (FGD, Female, 40+, Abidjan, June 26, 2010; Observations, Abidjan, 28 June 2010).

Perhaps, the acquisition of the *'card identete'*, which is basically the creation of the state, has been factored by the peculiarities of the Ivorian 'social space' as a 'country of migrants'. As such, it has been made a potent denominator for realizing individual and collective transnational intents (and interests) within the Ivorian 'social space'.

Identity Dualism as Impetus for Regional Integration and Development in West Africa

The process of simultaneous identification with two societies, as being played out by the Ejigbo-Yoruba in the course of their transnational engagements along the Nigerian-Ivorian corridor, seems to be presenting a positive framework for realizing the much desired integration and, of course, development within the West Africa sub-region. For instance, among the relatively older, returnee-indigenes of Ejigbo community in Nigeria (that is, 70 years and above), their retirement or relocation from Cote d'Ivoire has not stopped them from going back to the country intermittently by road despite the tedium and risk of the trip, especially for the elderly. Why? One, their existence is still largely tied to Cote d'Ivoire. They do go there to collect rents on their houses, shops and other business ventures (often managed by their Ivorian spouses or children or relatives who they took there *ab initio*). Some even go there to collect their retirement benefits and/or pensions from the Ivorian government (Observations, Ejigbo, Nigeria, 18 June 2010; Abidjan, Côte d'Ivoire, 21 June–2 July 2010).

Two, to visit their Ivorian friends whom they must have met in the course of their sojourn in Cote d'Ivoire, especially those who, one way or the other, facilitated the path of their existence while there; for instance, in the process of acquiring Ivorian residence permit, right of stay or citizenship, getting jobs and/or contracts, securing lands and/or property, marrying indigenes and, of course, in acquiring local spiritual power (Observations, Ejigbo, 18 June 2010; Abidjan, 21 June - 2 July 2010).

> .....I am on my way to collect rent on my house and shops in Abobo-Abidjan (Cote d'Ivoire) so that I could complete my house at Ejigbo (Nigeria)....I also want to do my annual pension verification....to visit my family and my old friend at Bouake to renew my 'gbetugbetu' (traditional spiritual power) which he gave me while we were working together in Abidjan (IDI, Male, Retiree, 86 years, 18 Ejigbo, June 2010).

Inferring from the text of the IDI above, it is conspicuous that the respondent, as applicable to others, still has arrays of reasons for sustaining his contact with the Ivorian society; from economic consideration to family consideration and, interestingly, 'spiritual' consideration. A conspicuous end product of all these interactions is the enhancement of possibility of integration across the ECOWAS region, though in a rather inverse pattern.

The nature of Ejigbo-Yoruba interactions with the Ivorian has prominently made both Ejigbo and Abidjan communities to become somewhat interdependent over the years. At the level of transactions, the *'Franc CFA'* has been a popular 'legal tender' in Ejigbo, and of course, exchanged with the *'Nigerian Naira'* in most households in the town. Reciprocally, this is the situation with the *'Nigerian Naira'* against the *'Franc CFA'* in most Nigerian households in Abidjan, often populated by the Ejigbo-Yoruba. Essentially, as many Ivorian commodities are sold in Ejigbo, so also identifiable local Nigerian commodities/items are retailed in Abidjan. Though, as a group in Abidjan, they tend to replicate most of the things done back home, there still exists a remarkable departure from the ideal. The Ivorian society has actually impacted on them. Therefore, a new outlook, definitely not wholly Ivorian or wholly Nigerian (possibly, ECOWAS) has emerged among them. The speaking pattern of the people has been largely distorted; whenever they speak Yoruba, colloquial Abidjan French usually reflects and vice versa (Observations, Ejigbo, 18 June 2010; Abidjan, 21 June –7 July 2010).

Conclusions

i) Enhanced integrative capability within the host society

The process of integrating migrants into the socio-economic workings of the 'host society' is usually better facilitated when the migrants' network is actively functioning at the centre of all migratory processes within the 'transnational social field' framework. That is, from the point of initiating the journey to the point of terminating the journey and, indeed, in the process of situating the migrants within the socio-economic specificities of the 'host' society, adequate involvement of the migrants' network has often tended to engender a functional integration process.

ii) Improved socio-economic and political participation within the host society

A productive integration of the migrants into the 'host' society will be a potent platform for enabling active functioning of the migrants within the socio-economic and political space of the 'host' society. For instance, social acceptability would always be a major avenue for facilitating economic participation; so also, a combination of both social acceptability and economic empowerment would encourage active political participation. Ostensibly, active political participation will be a veritable platform for engendering durable socio-economic integration of the migrants' community within the 'host' society.

iii) Prevalence of cross-cultural marriages between the migrants and their host

Between the migrants' community and the 'host' community, the prevalence of inter-marriage has tended to bolster the migratory trend and the process of integrating migrants within the 'host' society. Such marital relationship will routinely present the migrants (and the migrants' community) with the much desired sense of 'belonging' in dealing with everyday challenges. Aside from providing the migrants with imperative leverage to subsist within the host social space, such sense of 'belonging' portrays a formidable platform to realizing the regional integrative intent of the Economic Community of West African States (ECOWAS).

iv) Sustenance of pre-migratory interactive patterns with the home front

The 'transnational social space' presents individual migrants with the opportunity of sustaining the pre-migratory interactive patterns. Through the network functioning, ably depicted by the network association and cross-border transporters, migrants are able to interact with the 'home front'; for instance, in sending goods and funds for projects at 'home', and in receiving information and prospective migrants from 'home'. Indeed, the migrants function as if they are within the same social space as their 'country of origin' since the channel of communication has not been severed in any significant manner. To a considerable extent, this development has been quite functional to the realization of most migrants' intent of convenient re-integration into the home country after their sojourn.

v) Sustainable network members' contributions to socio-economic growth of both 'host' and 'home' societies

The patterns of interaction and interposition between the point of initiating migration and the process of integrating migrants within the 'host society' have given sufficient space for productive development outcomes. Between the two migratory poles, that is, the point of embarkation and the point of disembarkation, the migrants contribute to the process of socio-economic integration and development. In virtually all sectors of the host country, they are active; businesses are nurtured, taxes are paid, houses are built and the progress of the society is basically seen as being paramount to the realization of their transnational aspirations. Hence, they are usually willing to contribute all that is feasible to a smooth operation of the adopted social space. On the other hand, they are involved in various personal and communal projects back home. They build houses, and equally put business ventures in place from time to time. They usually embark on such projects in anticipation of the day they would have to stop functioning within the 'transnational social space' and return home.

iv) Facilitation of the larger regional integration and development agenda

The pattern of interaction, especially as it pertains to the process of identity positioning within the 'host society' has been of a significant impetus to the ongoing intent of the Economic Community of West African States (ECOWAS) to transform the regional body to an 'ECOWAS of People', in which all pertinent impediments towards regional integration will become obliterated. Such hindrances have included the language barrier, which the process of integration of migrants within the 'host society' has adequately taken care of. Of course, there cannot be proper integration without overcoming extant challenge of language diversity, first and foremost. Meanwhile, the integrative process of adequate positioning within the 'host society' has not been detrimental to the existing pre-migratory attachment of the migrants to their country of origin. As they are subsisting within the 'new environment', so also they are in intermittent touch with their kinsmen left behind in their 'home country'. When such micro trans-border interactive pattern is made sustainable, conveniently the process of socio-economic integration, and indeed, development at the larger regional level would become progressively oiled.

Recommendations

Inferring from the findings emanating from the entire study, it has been ostensible that from the point of initiating the journey to the point of arriving at the destination; till the last day of departure, the migrants' network has always been there for the Ejigbo-Yoruba migrants in Cote d'Ivoire. Therefore, in the process of identity construction within the Ivorian social space, individual migrants from Ejigbo, Nigeria, routinely carry the network group along. The individual's identity (identities) is oftentimes the network identity (identities); such identities so emanating are primarily geared towards the realization of related transnational goals of network members.

On the basis of the study's findings, the following recommendations have been deemed expedient for policy planners, network members and groups, and for the purpose of further research in related areas of research sojourn:

i) The functionality of 'transnational subsistence dualism', as practised by the Ejigbo-Yoruba migrants along the Nigerian-Ivorian migratory corridor, should be utilized as a veritable platform for fast-tracking the process of regional integration and development within the West African sub-region. Such extent of utilization has become more expedient in view of the ongoing intent of the ECOWAS authorities to transmute the regional body from 'an ECOWAS of States to an ECOWAS of People', in which the obstacles on the path of regional integration would be obliterated.

ii) Greater attention should be given to contextualizing the preference of the Ejigbo-Yoruba for migrating to Cote d'Ivoire despite prevalent colonial and contemporary impediments like language and related cultural specificities. Between Nigeria and Cote d'Ivoire, there exists Benin Republic, Togo and Ghana, and still the Ejigbo-Yoruba have enjoyed migrating to Cote d'Ivoire. Equally, the *lingua franca* in Cote d'Ivoire (that is, French) is not the same as that of Nigeria, which is English. Even none of the indigenous languages on either side is similar. Yet, the migration system on the Nigerian-Ivorian corridor has been bolstering. With further interest in this subject-matter, perhaps such unusual pattern of migratory practice could be utilized in explaining the process of regional integration as desired by the ECOWAS region.

iii) Essentially, the subsisting network group and the Oba's institution should be strengthened further in order to facilitate the course of the people's transnational engagements better. Over the years, this network group that has the institution of the 'Oba' as its central symbol has been quite functional in the growth, development and sustenance of the familial/kinship pattern, which has been driving the functioning of the network system since inception. Through the network platform, development ideas on both sides of the divide have often come to reality, especially those that are communal-based.

Also, in the process of carrying the migrants' community along, the Ivorian authorities have always found the network group, ably represented by the institution of the Oba, as a useful platform; more particularly in attaining social control amongst network migrants.

iv) The network identity should continue to take pre-eminence over individuals' identity within the transnational framework so as to make the process of integration sustainable, and of course, competition from other migrants' communities surmountable within the host society. The network identity, which seeks to integrate network migrants into the socio-economic workings of the host community and, at the same time, facilitating the sustenance of the pre-migratory relations with the home front, seems to have been functional, and indeed, productive over the years. The network identity has been tested; it has been sustainable over time and space. More significantly, the much desired leverage over other migrants' groups, especially those from other countries in West Africa is better attainable within the network framework. For instance, in the process of seeking economic space within the host society, such as shops, jobs, loans, contracts *et cetera*, the network group usually deploys the prevalent social capital amidst them such as interpersonal ties in the process. The result has, oftentimes, been more fruitful for individual network members in particular and the network group as a whole.

v) Communal and regional integration, and indeed, development should be fostered through the Ejigbo-Yoruba migratory experience along the Nigerian-Ivorian corridor. Within the framework of ongoing interaction between the Ejigbo-Yoruba migrants and the Ivorian society, both communal and regional integration and development could be attained. While communal development is noted to be taking place across the border already, the much needed regional integration could be facilitated if all subsisting impediments, as border posts and national policies that are often conflicting to the regional integrative interests, are considerably exorcised. As such, development of the region could be facilitated. This is deemed more necessary at this point, considering the subsisting transformational preference of the ECOWAS for an 'ECOWAS of People', in which 'free movement of people, goods and rights of establishment' will be prominently enabled instead of the usual 'ECOWAS of States', in which regional integration and development has been largely elusive.

References

Abba, A.I., 1993, 'The Niger factor in the implementation of Kano's policy on Almajirai', in Asiwaju, A.I. and Barkindo, B.M. eds, The Nigeria-Niger, A.I. Asiwaju and B.M. Barkindo, eds, in *The Niger-Nigeria Trans-Border Cooperation*, Lagos, Malthouse, pp. 390-396.

Adegbola, O., 1972, 'The Impact of Migration on the Rural Economy of Osun Division of Western Nigeria', Unpublished PhD Dissertation, Department of Geography, University of Ibadan, Ibadan, Nigeria.

Adeniran, I.A., 2009, 'Yoruba Wars of 19th Century', in Immanuel Ness, ed., *The International Encyclopedia of Revolution and Protest: 1500 to the Present*, Oxford, Wiley-Blackwell, pp. 3676-3678.

Adepoju, A., 2006, 'Internal and International Migration within Africa', in P. Kok, D. Gelderbloom, J.O. Oucha and J. van Zyl, eds, *Migration in South and Southern Africa: Dynamics and Determinants*, Cape Town, HSRC Press, pp. 26-45.

Afolayan, A.A., 1998, 'Immigration and Expulsion of ECOWAS Aliens in Nigeria', in *International Migration Review*, Vol. 22, pp. 4-27.

Afolayan, A.A., 2004, 'Circulatory Migration in West Africa: A Case Study of Ejigbo in South Western Nigeria', *L'Harmattan,* Paris, pp. 17-66.

Akinjogbin, I.A., 1980, 'The Economic Foundations of the Oyo Empire', in I.A. Akinjogbin, and S.O. Osoba, eds, *Ife History Series: Topics on Nigerian Economic and Social History*, Ile-Ife, University of Ife Press.

Alkali, M.N., 1985, 'Some Contributions to the Study of Pilgrimage Tradition in Nigeria', in *Annals of Borno*, Vol. II, pp. 127-138.

Asiwaju, A.I., 1992, 'West African History: The Significance for the Consolidation of ECOWAS', Paper presented at the National Seminar on Research Priorities and Integration in ECOWAS, Nigerian Institute of International Affairs, Lagos, 27-28 February. ECOWAS, 2010, Symposium on Regional Development, Ouagadougou, Burkina Faso, October.

Human Development Report, 2009, *United Nations Development Programme.*

Kivisto, P. and Faist, T., 2010, *Beyond a Border: The Causes and Consequences of Contemporary Immigration*, Thousand Oaks: Sage Publications.

Lawan, M., 2004, *No Travel is Little* (translated), Maiduguri, Sterpro, 3rd Edition.

Lee, E., 1966, *A Theory of Migration, Demography*, Vol. 3, No.1, pp. 47-57.

Mahadi, A., 1989, 'The Roles of Neighbouring Countries in the Nigerian Civil War', in T.N. Tamuno and S.C. Ukpabi, eds, *Nigeria since Independence: The First 25 years*, VVol. VI, pp. 252-276.

Richards, W. and Seary, A., 2000, 'Eigen Analysis of Networks', in *Journal of Social Structure*, September.

Tilly, C., 1996, 'What Good is Urban History?', in *Journal of Urban History*, Vol. 22, No. 6, pp. 702-719.

Manning, P., 2005, *Migration in World History*, New York and London: Routeledge.

Internet Sources

http://brown.edu/Faculties/Haffenreffer/yoruba2.html, accessed on 06/08/2011

http://un.org/Depts/Cartographic/map/profiles/westafrica.pdf, accessed on 06/08/2011

7

Children's Decision-making Mechanism to Migrate for work: Theoretical Analysis Applied to West Africa

Kabran Aristide Djane

Introduction

Child labour in the West African sub-region is of serious policy concern that transcends the square of mainstream social science. Indeed, most theories of child labour have affirmed that several factors do motivate children to migrate to identifiable agricultural and economic units. Since economic incentives usually draw the children, such unhealthy development for the children could be linked directly to the parents. As Diallo (2000) has suggested, many factors routinely engender the phenomenon of child labour. Among such are the socio-cultural, environmental (social norms), dysfunctional credit markets, household poverty, the weaknesses of the education system and legislative factors. Nevertheless, very negligible research works have addressed the reasons for children migrating to work in other countries in Africa. Such gap in knowledge is considered a potent theoretical issue that deserves a detailed epistemological explanation. Interestingly, the scope of the CODESRIA's Institute for Children (2011) has included issues bordering on how decisions are made in the process of children entering into related transnational practice. However, its transnational connotation in a globalized environment and implications for the regional integration process in West Africa, albeit Africa, deserves better attention than is being focused on in this chapter.

Contextualizing the African Child

A child in most legal definitions is any individual under the age of 18 years. Another broad category inevitably raises the Child and Adolescent classification, in measures of their needs and abilities (Hashim & Dorte 2011). This is essentially indicative of the fact that childhood entails a dynamic transformation of a child, in the aspects of physical, psychological and environmental composites. Erny (1987) in his analysis of the 'African child' also incorporates the spiritual dimension in his conceptualization of the child. This initiatory dimension plunges African children in the shelter of socialization within the community and allows them to live with these realities as adults. Thus, as the African child grows, he/she is subjected to the laws which govern the whole society. Hence, the child is prone to involvement in specific functions (Erny 1987:122). The African child in the Africanist design can then be required early to perform social or economic functions within the household or societal frameworks. This viewpoint has been captured by Kenyatta (1960:107): 'far from being a burden, the (African) child is a valuable aid, benefit, a necessity. Thus, the role of the child as a producer is more important than the productivity of farmers, and it is necessary to multiply planting operations, to maintain performance' (Lacoste 1968:30).

Children and Work in the African Context

Bonnet (1993:411) asks, 'what work, at what age children?' he answers thus: that the legislation in each African country, prohibits child labour and submits to strict protection. Also, Bonnet (1993) has been insistent on the fact that such legislation does not favour the industrial sector while children in sub-Saharan Africa, particularly in West Africa, do business in countries where so-called family or domestic work, and agriculture are very popular.

As a whole, the work of the child in the African context may be defined as any activity in different occupations other than the child's school work and all that the child could consider as play or games (Bonnet 1993). In 1998, the International Labour Conference, at its 86th Session, adopted the Internal Labour Organization (ILO) 'Declaration on Fundamental Principles and Rights at Work', which confirms that effective abolition of child labour is one of the fundamental principles that must be respected by all member-states of the ILO. While most of the countries in the West African sub-region function as members of the ILO, they have unduly allowed child labour to continue to thrive within their respective jurisdictions. Two dimensions in the definition of children have been strongly advocated by various international organizations, such as The United Nations Children's Fund (UNICEF) and the ILO; that is life in rural areas and the number of hours spent in a field. This second definition focuses on the variable of rural child labour.

In West Africa, the phenomenon of child labour could be empirically situated within four contexts depending on the quality of work: domestic work, work in career of begging, sex work and active participant in armed conflict. But Bonnet (1993) assures that the concept of 'work' in itself cannot be universalized because ethnographic approaches rely heavily on those who define it. But in all cases, Hashim & Dorte (2011) show a myriad of tasks performed by children around the world, and in West Africa in particular. Boys and girls are involved in agricultural and domestic work (Abede 2007; Katz 2004; Reynolds, Nieuwenhuys & Hanson 2006).

Regions of Strong Attraction for Child Labourers in West Africa

In the West African sub-region, the issue of child labour is economically built around the agricultural production areas and the urban centres. Most agricultural regions saw the emergence of children cross-border labour migrants during the boom period of the 1930s (that is, when the production of coffee and cocoa became unusually lucrative). Thus, Ghana and Côte d'Ivoire assumed the position of concentration for migrant children, who either moved with their parents or alone. As the economic boom advanced both Côte d'Ivoire and Ghana began experiencing the influx of child labourers from Burkina Faso, Mali and Niger Republic. It is worth noting that regional differentials were significant within the countries releasing child labourers. For instance, in Burkina Faso, Bisa Province in Boulgou Region has recorded the highest number of child labour migrants. This province has the lowest income level in the country – 82.7 FCFA per day (National Institute of Statistics and Demography of Burkina Faso 2008). In Ghana, the North-East has been heavily involved in the provision of child migrants in search of work. It is also the region with very low income level in the country (Porter and Canagarajah 2002).

The receiving areas are usually the rural centres in the destination countries where agricultural production is done on a mechanized scale. It is important to note that the migratory behaviour of children in West Africa has been following the established colonial tradition. Thus, despite the civil war in Côte d'Ivoire from 2002 to 2011, the country continued to receive migrants (including under-age ward labourers) from Burkina Faso in search of work in the cocoa producing regions of the country, such as Soubré, Daloa and Abengourou. The flow of migrant children, alone or accompanied, has strongly increased in the years following the devaluation of the CFA franc. Farmers from most Sahel countries were forced to migrate southward in search of a better living with their offspring. It is in this context that the individual decision to migrate becomes problematic because various factors that cut across political, social, cultural and economic are involved.

At another realm, if the history of migration in West Africa has been indicative of an increased monetized process and sustained financial exchanges between various actors in the migration system (Cordell & Al 1996), the system has been largely facilitated by cross-border intermediaries who have made the operation of the network a profession. Indeed, the development of agricultural areas related to coffee-cocoa has for decades sustained a migration pattern of individuals who have been seeking for better life (Grootaert & Kanbur 1995). The issue of concern now is: what is the appropriate age for an individual to decide to migrate for work across the border? Various scholars on migration research have suggested that the age at first migration for economic activity has been dwindling over the years, sometimes reaching infancy. Although, the decision by child labourers to migrate, in the West African sub-region, has in most cases been made by the parents or the family members, the ability to contribute to household sustenance at the point of origin of the migration has sustained the migratory process (Lambert 2007). Also, the social model that emphasizes the prominence of the family and the community in children migration has affirmed inexorably the capability of all age groups to contribute economically to the development of the society (Agarwal & Al 1997). It has also indicated that in some cases the decision to migrate has structurally been constructed around an economic logic which is now maintained by social intermediaries ranging from the near (relatives) to commission (Beauchemin 1999). The migration trajectory of children is then constructed from instruments developed by economic agents who observe the movement of children; hence, a cost-effective economic system perpetuates this child migration (Hasnat 1995).

Trajectory of Motivation and of Decision by Child Labourers to Migrate for Work

Although some children are driven to work due to neglect and family debt bondage, most of them do enter into it on their own volition (King 2002). Oftentimes, most children do take the decision to work for all sorts of reasons: to ensure the survival of the family; or when they are orphaned or living on the street, for their own survival; to escape the boredom of school, because they did not want to go there or because they are mistreated; to escape unbearable family situations; to have the money to buy anything from branded clothes to drugs; tor simply to feel independent (Sheller & Urry 2006).

Table 1: Child labour – level causal

Immediate causes	Underlying causes	Structural causes
Little or no money or food reserve	Disintegration of the extended family and informal social protection systems	Low national income
Family debt	Lack of parental education, high fertility rate	Inequality between countries and regions, unfavorable terms of trade
Increased prices of first necessity	Social aspiration for children, work and education	Incidence of crisis, war, financial or economic shocks, transition, HIV-AIDS
Non-existent school, poor or inappropriate facilities	Discrimination based on sex, caste, ethnicity, nationality etc.	Insufficient financial and political commitment to education, basic services and social protection (i.e. "bad governance")
Demand for cheap labor in the informal micro-enterprises	Consciousness of being poor: the desire to access consumption and a better standard of living	Social exclusion of the marginalized groups
The business or the family farm does not have the means to hire a employees	Children feel responsible for the family, and the "rich" for the poor	Lack of decent work for adults

Source: ILO (2002, p. 54)

Meanwhile, various models of parental choice, based on the idea that parents or other adults do decide for children to enter into the world of work rather than attend school, have assumed that such decisions are routinely motivated by rational economic criteria, selfish reasons or by outright ignorance (Elson 1982).

Thus, the term 'voluntary mobility' means that the child decides to move, sometimes against the will and without the consent of his parents. Between the voluntary act expressing an autonomous decision and submission to coercion or being forced to leave (forced mobility), several situations may arise (Terre des Hommes 2011). They are particularly influenced by the consent that reflects the spontaneous proposal from other children. In such case, the child grows up to give the consent. The idea did not come to him/her at first, but it eventually belongs to him/her.

Integration Implications of Child Labour Migration in West Africa

The West African sub-region comprises various countries, which are constituted by numerous ethnic groups. As such, the social, political, cultural and economic compositions of various countries differ. This means that the interpretation of the phenomenon of child labour in Nigeria differs from that of Senegal. Even within a given country, the realities of the communities are not always identical. It is therefore important to devise and support processes that enable communities to analyse and consider the best interests of their children in terms of their work, the education they receive, which will essentially structure their future and the choices and resources that will be available to them (Hashim 2007).

Various researches conducted by the African Movement of Working Children and Youth (AMWCY) on migration, trafficking, exploitation and abuse of children in the communities of West Africa focus on the difficulties in transcribing commonly used terms in international conventions into local languages and emphasizes the need to better understand the communities (Terre des Hommes 2011).

The United Nations has indicated that if the mobility of children cannot be tackled in its entirety, it must be accompanied by a protective collaboration between different states of West Africa. However, such collaboration has been near impossible across time and space due to differing laws and representations relating to child labour in different communities in West Africa. Hence, awareness of areas of origin, transit and destination according to the UNICEF may have more leverage in the fight against child labour (Whitehead, Hashim & Iverson 2007).

Conclusion

This chapter has specifically interrogated the process of decision-making in the entrance of children into the labour market in West Africa. It has observed that child labour is built economically around various production areas in the agricultural and urban centres in West Africa. Various agricultural regions saw the emergence of child labourers during the boom period of the 1930s (that is the production of coffee and cocoa). It has identified both Ghana and Côte d'Ivoire as the major countries of concentration of migrant child labourers within the sub-region. Such

migrant child labourers either come with their parents or on their own volition for
work. A specific multiplier effect of this development is that courtesy of related
intermingling of migrant children and the indigenous children, over time and space,
cultural boundaries are becoming obliterated. As such, regional integration is being
enhanced within the sub-region.

References

Abede, T., 2007, 'Changing livelihoods, changing childhoods: patterns of children's work in
    rural southern Ethiopia', *Children's Geographies* , 5 (1), 77-93.

Agarwal, S., Attah, M. & Kwakye, E.A., 1997, 'Bearing the weight: the Kayayoo, Ghana's
    working girl child', *International social work*, 40 (3): 425-463.

Beauchemin, E., 1999, 'The exodus: the growing migration of children from Ghana's rural
    areas to the urban centres', Accra: Catholic Action for street children (CAS) and UNICEF.

Bhalotra, S. & Heady, C., 1998, 'Child Labour in Rural Pakistan and Ghana:Myths and Data',
    Working paper, Department of Economics University of Bristol.

BIT, 2002, *UN Avenir sans travail des enfants*, Genève: Bureau International du Travail.

Bonnet, M., 1993, 'Le travail des enfants en Afrique', *Revue Internationale du Travail*, 411-430.

Canagarajah, S. & Pörtner, C., 2002, *Evolution of poverty and welfare in Ghana in the 1990's:
    achievements and challenges*, Washington, African Region Working Paper Series.

Cordell, D., Gregory, J. & Piche, V., 1996, *Hoe and wage: A Social History of a circular migration
    system in west Africa*, Boulder, Westview Press.

Diallo, Y., 2000, 'Les déterminants du travail des enfants en Côte d'Ivoire', *Centre d'économie
    du développement*.

Elson, D., 1982, 'The Differentiation of Children's Labour in the Capitalist Labour Market',
    Developement and Change, 13 (4): 479-498.

Erny, P., 1987, *L'enfant et son milieu en Afrique Noire*, Paris, L'harmattan.

Grootaert, C., & Kanbur, R., 1995, 'Child labor- an economic perspective', *International
    Labour Review*, 134 (2): 187-203.

Hashim, I., 2007, 'Independant child migration and education in Ghana', *Development and
    Change*, 38 (5): 911-931.

Hashim, I. & Dorte, T., 2011, *Child Migration in Africa*, Uppsala: Zed Books.

Hasnat, B., 1995, 'International trade and child labour', *Journal of Economic Issues*, XXXIX
    (2): 419-426

Imorou, A.B., 2008, *Le Coton et la Mobilité: les implications d'une culture de rente sur les trajectoires
    sociales des jeunes et enfants du Nord-Benin*, Dakar, Plan-Waro, Terre des Hommes et Lasdel-
    Benin.

INSD, 2008, *Enquête nationale sur le travail des enfants au Burkina-Faso*. Ouagadougou, Institut
    National de la Statistique et de la Demographie.

Katz, C., 2004, *Growing Up Global: Economic and Children's Everyday Lives*. Minnesota, University
    of Minnesota Press.

Kenyatta, J., 1960, *Au pied du Mont Kenya*, Paris, Maspero.

King, R., 2002, 'Towards a new map of European migration', *International Journal of Population
    Geography*, 8 (2): 89-106.

Lacoste, Y., 1968, 'Un problème carrefour dans les pays sous-développées: la signification économique de l'enfant, *Les carnets de l'enfance, UNICEF,* 7, 22-37.

Lambert, M., 2007, 'Politics, patriarchy, and the new traditions understanding female migration among the Jola (Senegal, West Africa)', in Dans H.P. Hahn & G. Klute, eds, *Cultures of Migration. African Perspectives* (pp. 129-148), Münster and Berlin, Lit Verlag.

Reynolds, P., Nieuwenhuys, O. & Hanson, K., 2006, 'Refractions of Childen's rights in development practice: a view from anthropology-introduction', *Childhood, 13* (3), 291-302.

Sheller, M. & Urry, J., 2006, 'The new mobilities paradigm', *Environmental and Planning A,* 38 (2) : 207-226.

TDH, 2011, 'Quelle protection pour les enfants concernés par la mobilité en Afrique de l'Ouest: Nos positions et recommandations', Dakar, Terre des Hommes.

Whitehead, A., Hashim, I. & Iverson, I., 2007, 'Child migration, child agency and inter-generational relations in Africa and South Africa', Working paper T24, Development Research Centre on Migration, Globalization and Poverty, University of Sussex.

8

Trans-border Banditry and Integration in the West African Sub-region

Olayinka Akanle and Ayokunle Olumuyiwa Omobowale

Introduction

Twenty-first-century West Africa within the Economic Community of West African States (ECOWAS) is best described as a period of the battle for integration. According to Olutayo, Olutayo and Akanle (2012), this is because regional integration has become a unique and distinctive characteristic of development efforts of nations in recent years. This explains why ECOWAS has struggled to change its focus from being just a body of *states* to being a body of *people*. The emphasis will be on integration drive and agenda for the ultimate advantage of the 15 member nations with a sense of nation-community for the over 300 million people making the ECOWAS region. This is against the realization that the orientation of community of people, rather than community of inanimate states that may not even recognize and accommodate the integration agenda, will ultimately drive the achievement of integration which is central to ECOWAS's vision. A lot of effort and attention have been directed at the integration subject within the commission and beyond. However, evidence on the ground shows that these have tended to be just mere rhetoric since effective actions have not matched the words especially in their actual consequences.

For example, according to Adeniran (2012), since the inception of the Commission, free movement of persons and goods within the sub-region is still a mirage traceable to incompatibilities in immigration and customs policies, monetary zones, and official languages among member states which have ultimately impeded positive integration within the ECOWAS framework. The ECOWAS drive for integration is to largely strengthen internal solidarity among member states to enable the body and the nations in the sub-region harmonize positions and articulate them as collective agenda within the global political economy where unity of purpose is fast becoming a necessity within global-regional bloc formations. The integration drive within the sub-region is necessarily the melting pot for the focus of ECOWAS. For instance, on the economic front, integration is to stimulate and fast-track the mechanism of a common market through free movement of commodities, markets, people and currency.

While the idea and practice of integration is noble and huge investments are placed on it in the sub-region through ECOWAS, trans-border banditry poses a huge threat to security and integration in the sub-region and this is a big paradox within a region and *community* with the goal of facilitating free movement of people without any clause. Acts of terrorism, armed robbery, cross-border sharing/trading of illegal arms and mercenaries are particularly real and endanger the integration of the ECOWAS region. In fact, since the establishment of ECOWAS on 28 May 1975 for the defence and development of the sub-region, never has trans-border banditry been as vehement as it is now. Of the 15 member states, many were either just coming out of crises or are still mired in crisis or are just about to be enveloped by it. The recipes and likelihood of crisis laden with trans-border banditry are rife. Cases of these abound but the cases of Sierra Leone, Liberia, Nigeria, Guinea Bissau and Mali are very important and worth noting as threats to the ECOWAS dream of collective vision of a peaceful, stable and economically prosperous and integrated sub-region. This also brings into focus the cases of trans-border banditry and robbery common along the Chad, Cameroun, Niger and Nigeria borders as will be shown below. Yet, while much have been written on the theory and practice of migration, free movement and integration in the ECOWAS sub-region, not much exists on the actual free movement of people and the elimination of trans-border banditry. At the same time, the cherished ideal of integration has largely remained elusive even when peace and security are fundamentally acknowledged as critical to ECOWAS, especially relative to the ultimate goal of sustainable development. It is against this backdrop that this chapter engages the problematic.

Banditry in the ECOWAS Sub-region: The Clustered Case Studies

This section of the chapter discusses the domains of major clusters of trans-border banditry in the ECOWAS sub-region. The main clusters are; aided rebellion, armed robbery and terrorism. Let us begin with aided rebellion in Mali.

The Case of Aided Rebellion

The case of Mali remains the most daunting threat to the very essence of ECOWAS. northern Mali has been hijacked by Islamic fundamentalists and Tuareg rebels and it is far out of control of the Malian Government and, in like sense, ECOWAS. Given the topography of Mali and incursion of Al-Qaeda coupled with the ultimate threat to the Mali state, resolution of the rebellion has become very problematic. This has been further compounded by the lukewarm attitude of Nigeria, who has the region's strongest army, to deploy troops in Mali. The Mali mission becomes even more complicated when other factors like the language barrier, the financial crunch and insurgency in Nigeria itself are taken into account. Given the Nigerian deployment challenge, it has also become evident that ECOWAS could not rush into action. This is why the French took the lead by deploying troops and air power in Mali; they have been reported as alluding to the unanticipated strength of the rebels. While the French originally deployed 1,500 military personnel in Mali and were ready to send more, Nigeria deployed an initial 900 while ECOWAS prepared for 3,000 troops (see Karimi 2013).

The rebellion in Mali has come to be popularly known as the Tuareg Rebellion of 2012 and it has covered the whole of northern Mali and has come very close to the capital which explains why the government demanded immediate international assistance. The Tuareg rebellion caught international attention for four main reasons: the involvement of Al-Qaeda, the trans-border involvement of other nationals from the West Africa (especially those who fought against the late Colonel Ghadaffi in Libya) and the colossal destruction of lives and property, destruction of historical sites, as well as wanton violation of human rights of the Malians. The world and ECOWAS did not interfere when it was totally a Malian affair but when it became trans-border in nature, ECOWAS had to pay attention especially as the international community and the United Nations Security Council had already indicated it would count on ECOWAS to take the lead. The Malian Rebellion threatened to destabilize the sub-region as the neighbouring nations were beginning to be adversely affected as seen in the cases of Niger, Senegal and Nigeria. The Malian mercenaries were moving in and out of Mali into and through the neighbouring nations, thus threatening their peace and security. Although the Malian crisis started as a war of independence against the Malian government in the Sahara desert region of Azawad as led by the National Movement for the Liberation of Azawad (MNLA), being part of insurgencies by traditionally nomadic Tuaregs beginning in the early twentieth century that were joined by the Islamist group Ansar Dine, it has since escalated beyond the local to that which now threatens regional and global peace due to the infiltration of opportunistic external and trans-border groups.

The trans-border dimension of the rebellion has made the crisis more difficult to resolve as it has assumed ethnic and sophisticated dimensions in terms of tactics, personnel and equipment. Socio-psychological trajectories as well as political undercurrents further complicate the crisis. Unfortunately, as it destabilizes the nation and the sub-region and further blacklists the continent as the *Dark Continent* and *the Continent of War*, lives and property of the ECOWAS nationals are being lost and this is grave when viewed in the context of the ECOWAS intent to become 'an ECOWAS of people'. For instance, due to the incessant attacks by the rebels and the government troops, the number of casualties has increased tremendously. Over 30,000 civilians remain internally displaced while many remain refugees in Mauritania and Niger (see UNHCR 2013). For instance, the United Nations High Commission for Refugees released figures on 4 April which showed a grim picture of the crisis. According to UNHCR, there are estimated 200,000 displaced persons in Mali with not less than 400 people desperately entering Burkina Faso and Mauritania per day for fear of being caught in the crossfire while hundreds have actually been killed in the crisis

(UNHCR 2013). It is, however, important to note that there are mostly *unaccounted for, displaced Malians* who are now burdened populations across West Africa. The Malian crisis has led to the proliferation of arms and armed groups, preponderance of violence and crimes; rape, murder, kidnapping, maiming and the phenomenon of child soldiers in the West African sub-region with huge negative consequences for the peace, security, integration and development of ECOWAS. The crisis has also led to the near collapse of the Malian state, destruction of the world heritage site, Timbuktu, and forceful imposition of Islamic Law *(Sharia)* on the people.

The Case of Terrorism: A Look at *Boko Haram*

Boko Haram means *western education* (civilization) *is a sin*. For this reason, members of the *Boko Haram* sect have a mandate among themselves to resist anything western, especially education, through whatever means including violence as a form of *jihad* (warfare in defence of Islam). *Boko Haram* is an Islamic sect that has held Nigeria hostage for years (since 2009) with no sign of resolution. In fact, the most formidable problem confronting Nigeria today after poverty is the *Boko Haram* insurgency. The insurgency has paralysed Northern Nigeria's economy and has destroyed the secure existence of the region while it has also strained the national security apparatuses. Reports by senior security officers claim a lot of *Boko Haram* foot soldiers come from countries contiguous with Nigeria in the West African sub-region. The main strategy of *Boko Haram* is violence and guerrilla warfare with the ultimate aim of Islamizing Nigeria or at least the North just as in Mali. Interestingly, just as in Mali, trans-border gangs and mercenaries drive the *Boko Haram* as fighters come and go through the Chad, Niger, Cameroun and other neighbouring countries.

It is also noted that, sometimes, the same set of mercenaries propel the Malian and *Boko Haram* crises as they move through the porous borders of the ECOWAS sub-region especially through the free movement of people protocol. Hence, when the people move across borders, they move with arms for intended crises as they unleash terror on unsuspecting innocent citizens they meet on their paths. Unfortunately, identifying the mercenaries physically is nearly impossible as they have no special features with which they could be identified and this is one of the reasons why it has become nearly impossible to resolve the *Boko Haram* problem. At the same time, the Islamization agenda has caught the fancy of other Muslims across the Maghreb which now support the *Boko Haram* as they have come to be seen as fighting a *Holy War* which they are ultimately part of. This accounts for their free movement through the porous sub-regional borders since 2009. While it is possible to see *Boko Haram* as a militant Islamic group fighting for *Sharia* in Nigeria, they have been declared a terrorist group in Nigeria and across the world (at least in principle).

Boko Haram target government officials and security forces to propagate their crusade against western education and its attributes. Although the target of *Boko Haram* is Nigeria, the epicentre is the widely Islamic north where the battle is fierce and the agenda most prevalent. The sociology of the northern epicentre of *Boko*

Haram is against the background that the northern socio-economic, political and cultural systems provide the most compatible base and structure for the *Boko Haram* agenda. Hence, while *Boko Haram* has been very strong in the north, especially in Borno, Yobe, Adamawa, Kano and Plateau states, the group has not been so *successful* in the south due to large socio-economic, political, geographical and cultural systems' incompatibilities. Generally, however, *Boko Haram* has been the most destructive in the modern history of Nigeria and among the most destructive, disintegrating and destabilizing in the modern history of the ECOWAS. Over 1,000 people have been killed through the terrorism of *Boko Haram* and millions of dollar worth of properties destroyed (Umar (2011).

The activities of *Boko Haram* have been recognized by ECOWAS at several meetings and the helplessness of the Nigerian government to tackle the issue sustainably has been acknowledged. This is why ECOWAS as a body and individual nations in the sub-region, including those out of ECOWAS like the United States of America and the United Kingdom, have offered assistance to Nigeria to curb the *Boko Haram* menace. Nigeria has however not taken advantage of these gestures of help as the government believes that will be an acceptance of its incapability to handle *Boko Haram*. The concern of ECOWAS, which is legitimate, is that the ascendancy of *Boko Haram* comes as a real threat to sub-regional peace and security and integration especially as *Boko Haram* fighters move trans-border to perpetrate their acts of terrorism. Every time they unleash mayhem, they claim responsibility across the world and see it as an achievement. Thus, the more collateral damage they do, the better for them and this is dangerous for the sub-region and the nation that prides itself as the Giant of Africa. Nigeria is the most populous nation in the sub-region. Thus, any problem that destabilizes the nation will certainly have grave consequences for the sub-region. That makes ECOWAS' concern with the *Boko Haram* terrorism quite legitimate.

The Case of Trans-border Armed Robbery

Trans-border Armed Robbery (which we call TAR here) is another case that is very common across the sub-region. Travellers, border town/village residents and traders are frequently robbed and attacked by armed robbers without any protection from law enforcement agents. Borders in the sub-region are either outright unpoliced or poorly policed, making them easy areas of operations for the hoodlums. Part of the reason is that there are no effective ECOWAS protocols to police borders, particularly against armed robbery. Yet, nations poorly cater for and hardly recognize border towns/villages in their security systems. Sometimes, such localities are seen as neither here nor there, except when they are in contention, especially when valuable mineral resources like crude oil are found in those places. Even at that, the interest is usually in the material resources rather than the people. ECOWAS border villages are thus at the mercy of faith and trans-border armed robbers as nations poorly account for the security of the border towns/villages.

Cases of TAR abound in ECOWAS but recent popular ones that occurred in the sub-region are worth mentioning. These are the trans-border robbery incidents in Potiskum, Plateau State and Adamawa. The Potiskum case was actually at the Potiskum cattle market and it was a reprisal attack which left over 50 people dead, most of them innocent cattle traders at the market. The incident occurred sequel to the killing of a trans-border armed robber caught after his gang escaped. The armed robbers then reinforced and attacked the defenceless traders, customers and cattle with sophisticated weapons and explosives in an obvious act of vengeance. The victims had little or no help from the security operatives responsible for the area. This incident was very bloody. These incidents should be of concern to ECOWAS as the robbers move unhindered across the borders of Chad, Cameroun and Niger (see African Examiner 2012) with arms and ammunition, to perpetrate their obnoxious acts, especially during market periods, ceremonies and any time of day.

Cases of trans-border armed robbery also frequently occur at the Sorou-Belel and Konkol communities in Maiha Local Government Area of Adamawa State, Nigeria, according to Muhammad (2010). The border communities in the northern part of the state are usually victims of trans-border armed robbery gangs, to the extent that the residents had to adjust their culture as coping strategies against armed robberies. A major part of the cultural adjustment, according to Muhammad (2010), is to appear poor even if rich, refusal to count money in public and never to splash money at traditional functions as these could invite armed robbers at any time when there is no protection from security agencies. Due to the failure of state security apparatuses in the area, the residents have instituted a local arrangement of securing themselves and their properties but these arrangements have been largely ineffective as the trans-border armed robbers are always more armed and sophisticated than the local security systems, which suggests the need for sub-regional and national security assistance. Robberies are frequent but are most likely on every market day when the robbers are sure of huge cash collections in the highly cash-oriented economy of the communities like in most African traditional societies with poor banking culture and without other cashless technologies. These communities border Cameroun and the armed robbers move in and out of the Republic of Cameroun and Nigeria to perpetrate their acts to the detriment of the rural people who have suffered scandalous neglect from both governments and ECOWAS. Trans-border armed robbery has, in recent times, accounted for about 30 deaths and many wounded. The casualties included police officers and civilians, not to mention millions of uninsured cash and property stolen at gunpoint by the trans-border armed robbers. The case of trans-border banditry around the Benin Republic/Lagos axis is also common and it has led to a number of diplomatic rows between the governments of Nigeria and Republic of Benin especially under the regime of President Olusegun Obasanjo due to the dare-devil robbery activities of the notorious armed robber, *Shina Rambo,* and many others not so popular but equally dangerous armed robbery gangs.

The Implications of Trans-border Banditry to Integration

As earlier stated, the integration of the peoples of the ECOWAS region remains the most laudable goal of the ECOWAS. As laudable as it is, it is threatened by insecurity occasioned by trans-border banditry (Miles 2005; Willet 2005). The recent happenings in Mali, in particular, present training ground for violent Islamic groups aiming to Islamize Nigeria and other ECOWAS states through jihad and introduce strict versions of the Sharia law. Islamists who have found a safe haven in northern Mali, seemingly proffer the agenda of 'integration through islamization' with serious implications to the peoples and cultures of the region. Across the western African coast there are diverse socio-demographic, economic and cultural groups whose ways of life, freedom and identities would be obliterated through forceful Islamization. Hence, the governments and citizens of other western African states justifiably view migrant Malians with suspicion as potential security threats. The welcoming trust, brotherliness and good neighbourliness which are the bedrock values of African people (Omobowale and Olutayo 2012), and are very germane for peoples' integration, are sacrificed for security reasons. An average Malian (especially) of northern origin becomes a potential security threat that must be handled with absolute caution. Whereas the average Malian does not necessarily belong to the brigandage violent religious sects, the activities of these religious sects threaten West African integration and security.

With huge weaponry and determination to run over not just Mali, but other contiguous countries, the Islamic insurgency in Mali potentially threatens peace in West Africa. Northern Mali without state control is a potential breeding ground for Al Qaeda and other terrorist organizations that could make the vast and difficult topography of the Sahara Desert a vantage terrain for them to thrive (Benjaminsen 2008; Gutelius 2007), plan, organize and launch attacks on other West Africa states. The recent French and Nigerian-led onslaught against northern Mali's Islamic insurgents notwithstanding, it is important to note that while the regular armies of these nations may have superior firepower, they may lack the adequate knowledgeof the desert topography to effectively rout the Islamist guerrilla army and totally annihilate them. They may retreat to their enclaves, to hide from the superior air and land weaponry of the advancing foreign regular armies. It is important to note that they retreat only to attack some other time. Besides, with support from renegade Islamist/terrorist groups along contiguous countries in North Africa, stretching up to the Middle-East, the power base of northern Malian insurgents may not be quickly weakened. What may be happening in the nearest future may be a continuation of eastern-western or Islamist-western proxy wars, in West Africa.

During the Cold War era, many proxy wars were fought in the Third World under the 'canopy' of opposing socialist and capitalist super powers that provided arms to warring sides (Barnes and Farish 2006; Omobowale and Olutayo 2005). The capitalist nations of the United States of America, Great Britain and France on one side, and the socialist state of USSR (Union of Soviet Socialist Republics) made money and proved their military arsenals on the battlefields of eastern Europe, Asia and Africa. The unfolding events in northern Mali may not be different after all. As the battle between the Islamists and the West spreads into West Africa, the West African sub-region economically and culturally disintegrates with grave consequences for the internal security of the West African states.

The *Boko Haram* insurgency in Nigeria is also partly fuelled by trans-border banditry (Onuoha 2010, Danjibo 2009). The common culture, language and religion across the northern tip of West Africa readily blend a people of diverse states, seemingly into common ancestry and brotherliness. Hence, Chadian, Nigerien and Malian migrants alongside other people, freely migrate into Nigeria. Reports claim that the ranks of *Boko Haram* foot soldiers and bombers are actually swelled by non-Nigerian migrants from Chad, Mali and Niger (Sahel Blog 2012) with common ancestry, culture and language with the peoples of northern Nigeria. Hence, the socio-cultural blend between migrants from countries contiguous with northern Nigeria, presents a security challenge for Nigeria whose citizens are exposed to attacks from *Boko Haram*. The mission of *Boko Haram* is simply congealed with those of the trans-border armed bandits who join the ranks of insurgent group to cause havoc in Nigeria.

The *Boko Haram* insurgency and its links to armed groups in countries along the borders of northern Nigeria threatens integration among ECOWAS states. The fear of *Boko Haram* and the spread of Islamic militancy into other African countries potentially portend an anti-migration policy to curtail the possible spread of *Boko Haram* to other countries along the West African coast. On the one hand, the integration of a people of common culture along the northern tip of West Africa, which unfortunately allows a blending into *Boko Haram* insurgency also possibly de-integrates West Africans as the people down south, especially in Nigeria, view Malian, Chadian and Nigerien with utmost suspicion and caution, seeing them as potential assailants. The fear is, of course, not far-fetched as there are speculations that Hausa and Fulani herders from countries along the borders of northern Nigeria cause mayhem along their pathways attacking villagers and destroying crops as they herd animals through northern and southern Nigeria. Many of the trans-border pastoralists are heavily armed herder-bandits, carrying AK 47 assault rifles as they move. The assumption is that they easily access arms because of the illegal free flow of firearms across West Africa's porous borders due to the many civil wars that the sub-continent has experienced over the last 20 years. Liberia, Sierra Leone, Mali, Niger, Chad and Cote d'Ivoire have all experienced civil wars lately and so it is not unlikely that armed bandits are able to access illegal arms from the armouries of former rebels which were not retrieved.

Equipped with assault guns and the technology and knowledge of making home-made explosive devices, *Boko Haram* poses a serious threat to the integration of West Africa's people. The diverse states have recognized integration in their 'letters' largely based on the tenets of the ECOWAS Charter. West Africans can travel within the West African region and stay for beyond 90 days without visas, provided they possess valid identification papers such as the ECOWAS passport (issued by each member state). Nevertheless, armed groups such as *Boko Haram* negate the ECOWAS 'one people' principle, as the activities of this group and its trans-border network engenders fear and suspicion in fellow West Africans. Finally, the nefarious activities of various trans-border armed groups along the West African corridor, including trans-border armed robbers, Islamic insurgents and *Boko Haram* present debilitating security challenges and are hinderances to the integration of the people of West Africa.

Conclusion

This chapter concludes that the ECOWAS' charter goal of integration of the West African people may not be achievable, after all, due to incessant trans-border banditry and attendant insecurity. Trans-border banditry would continue to de-integrate the people of the sub-continent who would continue to harbour mutual suspicion and mistrust as armed groups inflict pain and destruction on lives and property.

References

Adeniran, B., 2012, 'Regional Integration in the ECOWAS Region: Challenges and Opportunities', *Backgrounder*, No. 19, Accessed at http://www.africaportal.org/articles/2012/01/17/regional-integration-ecowas-region-challenges-and-opportunities.16 January 2013.

African Examiner, 2012, Armed Bandits kill 60, burn down Nigeria's

Barnes, T.J. and Farish, M., 2006, 'Between Regions: Science, Militarism, and American Geography from World War to Cold War', *Annals of the Association of American Geographers* 96 (4): 807-826.

Benjaminsen, T.A., 2008, 'Does Supply-Induced Scarcity Drive Violent Conflicts in the African Sahel? The Case of the Tuareg Rebellion in Northern Mali', *Journal of Peace Research* 45 (6): 819-836.

Danjibo, N.D., 2009, 'Islamic Fundamentalism and Sectarian Violence: The "Maitatsine" and "Boko Haram" Crises in Northern Nigeria', Peace and Conflict Studies Paper Series, 2009 - ifra-nigeria.org accessed on 22 January 2013 from https://ifra-nigeria.org/IMG/pdf/N-_D-_DANJIBO_-_Islamic_Fundamentalism_and_Sectarian_Violence_The_Maitatsine_and_Boko_Haram_Crises_in_Northern_Nigeria.pdf.

Gutelius, D., 2007, 'Islam in Northern Mali and the War on Terror', *Journal of Contemporary African Studies* 25 (1): 59-76.

Karimi, F., 2013, 'Malian rebels vow to 'open gates of hell' as U.S. weighs policy options', Accessed at http://edition.cnn.com/2013/01/16/world/africa/us-mali-military/index.html 29 January 2013.

Miles, W.F.S., 2005, 'Development, Not Division: Local versus External Perceptions of the Niger-Nigeria Boundary', *The Journal of Modern African Studies*, Vol. 43, No. 2 (June), pp. 297-320.

Muhammad, I., 2010, 'Adamawa borders: Where residents daren't count money openly', http://weeklytrust.com.ng/index.php?option=com_content&view=article&id=4774:adamawa-borders-where-residents-darent-count-money-openly&catid=41:news&Itemid=30, Accessed 16 January 2013.

Olutayo, A.O., Olutayo, M.A.O. & Akanle, O., 2012, *The New Strategic Approaches to Integration and Development in the Economic Community of West African States (ECOWAS) region: towards securing the future*, Ebook, L'Harmattan. http://www.editions-harmattan.fr/index.asp?navig=catalogue&obj=article&no=24505. Accessed 17 January 2012.

Omobowale, A.O. and Olutayo A.O., 2005, 'Globalisation, Governance and Armed Conflict in Africa', *African Journal for the Psychological Study of Social Issues* 8 (1&2): 58-72.

Omobowale, A.O. and Olutayo, A.O., 2012, 'Culture and Development' in S.C. Madubuike, ed., *Ethnography of Culture and Civilization in Africa*, Ibadan, Agbo Areo Publishers, pp. 59-79.

Onuoha, F.C., 2010, 'The Islamist challenge: Nigeria's Boko Haram crisis explained', *African Security Review*, 19 (2): 54-67.

Potiskum cattle market', http://africanexaminer.com/cattle0504, Accessed 16th January, 2013.

Umar, S., 2011, *The Discourses of Salafi Radicalism and Salafi Counter-radicalism in Nigeria : A Case-study of Boko Haram*, Northwestern University.

United Nations High Commission for Refugees (UNHCR), 2013, *2013 UNHCR Country Operations Profile - Mali Situation (Mali, Niger, Burkina Faso)*, Accessed 29 January 2013 at http://www.unhcr.org/pages/49e484e66.html

Willett, S., 2005, 'New Barbarians at the Gate: Losing the Liberal Peace in Africa', *Review of African Political Economy*, 32 (106): 569-594

9

From State Back to the State: Lessons for ECOWAS Countries

A.O. Olutayo, Olayinka Akanle and M.A.O Olutayo

Introduction

The essence of all activities of a state and across states is to ensure human development; that is, to guarantee a process through which peoples' choices and the capacities to make such choices are enlarged. This is because of the understanding that capacities to make such choices will ensure long, healthy life, positive standard of living and create conducive environments for people as individuals and as groups to develop their full potentials and have appreciable life chances that would make existence worthwhile. Interestingly, this is a win-win situation for all; rich or poor, the ruled and the rulers, north or south or whatever the dichotomy is. Ordinarily against this background, development should be easy. And it should be desirable. Unfortunately, while human development is desirable for many in sub-Saharan Africa, the region is mostly in discourse for its scandalous underdevelopment. According to Boafo-Arthur (2003), the region hits international news headlines only in the context of natural disasters, conflicts, wars, poverty *and maladministration* (emphasis ours). Regrettably, everyone becomes a development expert where the issue of Africa's development is concerned. The orientation relative to African sub-Saharan development debate is that 'we all do development'. Everyone assumes development orthodoxy relative to the region, making the region a confused, suffocating and ineffective development laboratory.

This is why Juma, in his paper presented at the 2006 Hilton Lecture of the Royal Academy of Engineering, maintained that 'development is easier done than said' (p.3). That was the first statement in the thought-provoking paper. Juma (2006) inversed the old maxim to reflect the end of an era in which sub-Saharan Africa's development was defined as an issue for public discourse rather than accomplishment. The call in the contemporary development circle is thus practical solutions to a challenging problem. Attention must of necessity shift from familiar discourses to radical approaches, to galvanize needed development in the region. Hitherto, most of the ideas, policies and efforts to jumpstart development in sub-Saharan Africa, with particular reference to the ECOWAS sates, were from without; such that policies and ideas were formulated, implemented and supervised from the West and by the West. The Western 'experts' foisted development ideas and policies on sub-Saharan Africa's governments, even military ones, and they enforced such policies with debilitating sanctions.

Attempts to decorate the policies to have local content or to appear to have originated within Africa, for the benefit of the Africans, did not help either. Critical reasoning would clearly show that the fundamental ideas behind the policies were from without and were principally for the benefit of the North. It is therefore not surprising that those policies largely failed in Africa and left the people poorer than they were prior to the implementation of the policies but not until they had enriched the initiators. The arrowhead of these imposed development paradigms was the Structural Adjustment Programmes (SAP hereinafter). SAP was all about rolling back the state to accelerate development of the states in Africa and elsewhere. It however succeeded only in creating more poverty and generalized underdevelopment. In fact, the gains and accelerated development in the immediate post-independence era in West Africa, like in most African countries were either *traded-off* or stagnated while despondency replaced hope as various countries are still struggling to come to terms with the hydra-headed consequences *of SAP* (Boafo-Arthur 2003) (emphasies ours).

Although disparity in growth rates and development indicators in the West African region continually generates debates on the actual level of development of member states, the fact of the matter is that no country in the ECOWAS region today is close to being categorized as developed as each country faces one debilitating development problem or the other. The problems member states face include expensive democracy, weak governments, compromised infrastructures, large-scale and life threatening corruption, wicked political elites, wars and over-dependence on external influence. The only signs of potential development viability in the ECOWAS region today are the gradual return to democracy and fairly stable governments. The overall success in the long run will, however, depend on the sustainability of even the positive signs; but time will tell as this is not the first time such signs have emerged in the region.

The traditional drive of SAP is that state influences must be replaced with free markets, deregulation and privatization, to ensure development. Experience has, however, shown otherwise. This is, first, because it has now been shown by the situation in the different states that SAP has failed its adopters. Second, it is because SAP is still being implemented in Arica under various guises. Reforms that are variants of SAP are still being implemented in states like Nigeria at a time when Venezuela is indigenizing its already privatized critical sectors. Hence, Nigeria is currently implementing privatization of its electricity, telecommunications and oil sector, just to mention a few, while Venezuela is forcefully, taking over already privatized public utilities when necessary, even against western condemnation and heavy propaganda. Radical approaches like those of Venezuela are discredited by neo-liberal apologists, but the failure by developing economies to jettison their dependence on the West could mean condemnation to underdevelopment and acceptance of the popular There is No Alternative (TINA) construct (Olutayo, Olutayo and Omobowale 2005; Boafo-Arthur 2003).

The aim of this chapter is to examine the development model of SAP relative to other models with implications for the development of West African states. Drawing from the lessons learnt from the trajectories of SAP in sub-Saharan Africa, the chapter suggests an alternative approach to achieving sustainable development in ECOWAS countries.

A Survey of the SAP Topography

The need for models and frameworks to engineer development can never be over-emphasized. Models guide state activities in achieving development. This is more so if such models have performed creditably well in other socio-economic, cultural and political jurisdictions. Against the performance considerations, most of such models are even adopted without painstaking operational content evaluations, while possible local options compliant with local dynamics are often supplanted under ideological barrage. Often, needed critical model and policy considerations are trivialized and reduced to rhetorical discussions and guided diplomatic discourses often designed by international development 'experts' marshalled by the World Bank and the International Monetary Fund (IMF) (the popular Bretton Woods institutions). Real and extensive development models and critical frameworks have been side-lined to the margins of international development over the years while the prescriptions from the Bretton Woods organizations have been adopted to the point of overdose and have taken the centre stage, as in the case of SAP.

The development experiences of South Korea and Taiwan formed the fundamental bases upon which the SAP was built by the World Bank and others (Taylor 2001). The two nations are commonly referred to as the twentieth century miracles and development success stories. Both countries shared identical experiences as underdeveloped nations and emerged as very close to the developed nations on important development indices of health, education and industrialization. On negative terms, development scenarios (underdevelopment), both nations commenced the 1950s with absolute poverty of most of their citizens, life expectancies were 56-60 years and both were encumbered with problems as colonies of Japan all through the first half of the century (Taylor 2001). Their success stories were, however, noticed with growth rates of 6 per cent to 8 per cent in their per capita Gross Domestic Products (GDPs) from the early 1960s to the 2000s.

More importantly, as against the development of the BRIC nations (Brazil, India and China), the development of South Korea and Taiwan had a trickle-down effect on the average people as the citizens enjoyed wage increase and appreciable living standard improvements with an equitable distribution of income identical to those of Japan, Holland and France. This is why these nations have often been described as bold, confident, resolute, daring and worthy of emulation in the global search for development. These characteristics have earned them such names and accolades as Asian Dragons, Asian Tigers and Contemporary Development Miracles. As already mentioned above, the Asian Tigers' experience largely informed the SAP thrust in developing countries in West Africa, as their development paths were carved in gold for other developing nations. These were strongly prescribed by the World Bank and the IMF. The implementation of SAP in sub-Saharan Africa was particularly easy because the economic situation in the region was precarious. SAP was thus introduced in the region in the 1980s. During this period, many African economies witnessed serious economic disruptions (Ayadi, Adegbite and Ayadi 2008) traceable to oil crises, poor commodity pricing and generalized negative effects of global shocks.

These resulted in collapsed currencies, external debts complications (Ayadi, Adegbite and Ayadi 2008) and aggravated imbalances in Foreign Direct Investments (FDIs). The background dynamics sent the vulnerable countries to the international organizations for assistance. Unfortunately, the international organizations required economic reforms in the toga of SAP as preconditions for financial assistance and bail. This was certainly punishment for looking without, rather than within, for solutions. In line with the Modernization Theory that proffers the development tracks of early developers to later ones as sure ways to development, SAP was foisted on African nations with little or no options, *ab initio*. SAP was offered by the Bretton Woods organizations as sure economic recovery initiative designed to rescue Africa from the doldrums of economic abyss it seemed to be sinking into (Olutayo and Omobowale 2005). If it was really to rescue Africa socioeconomically, SAP should be welcomed as a messianic development by all (Olutayo and Omobowale 2005); but this was not to be, as the socioeconomically debilitating effects were crucifying.

The SAP was implemented in the African countries to restructure and diversify the productive base of the economies to reduce dependency on the oil sector and imports, achieve fiscal and balance of payment viability on the medium term and to promote non-inflationary economic growth. Against these broad objectives, African nations designed policies to achieve development within the SAP framework. For example, in order to legalize the agenda for reforms in Nigeria, the federal government promulgated the Privatization and Commercialization Decree No. 25 of 1988 and the Programme for the Implementation of the Provisions of the decree was initially coordinated and supervised by the Technical Committee on Privatization and Commercialization (TCPC), now the Bureau for Public Enterprises (BPE) (Ibeabuchi, Essien, Appah and Idowu 2003). Against public outcry and criticisms, the Decree No. 25 of 1988 and the general SAP framework, in Nigeria like other states in the region, had the following objectives:

- Reducing the size and scope of government through restructuring and rationalization to lessen the dominance of unproductive investments in public enterprises.
- Refocusing the enterprises slated for privatization to enhance performance, viability and overall efficiency, promoting a favourable climate for domestic

investment and creating a positive attitude towards private investment for both local and foreign entrepreneurs.

- Promoting equity ownership among employees of privatized businesses in order to motivate them towards higher productivity.
- Providing consumers with improved services, better product quality, wider choices, new products and lower prices.
- Improving the profitability of the privatized firms through competition (Ibeabuchi, Essien, Appah and Idowu 2003).
- Strengthening of hitherto strong and relevant demand management policies.
- Adoption of measures to stimulate domestic production and broaden the supply base of the economy.
- Setting up of a Second-Tier Foreign Exchange Market (SFEM) to ensure 'realistic' exchange rate to guarantee efficient resources allocation and promote domestic balanced production and non-oil exports.
- Industrial diversification.
- Liberalization of external trade and payments system fluidity as well as prices, trade and exchange control elimination.
- The elimination of price controls and commodity boards.
- The decontrol of interest rates.

The SAP implementation policy arrangements adopted by all West African states are largely identical. From the above policy lists, ECOWAS member states fit in excellently as they wiggle through the burden of SAP. States mostly approached SAP through a total reform of the economy; and they took on too many reforms at the same time beyond their capacities, within a short time under poor policy guidelines supervised by the many international experts. The combined effects of poor policy, weak guidelines, negative governments and states' capacities, corruption, policy reversals and poor infrastructures consequently created more development problems for the African nations than were could be solved *ab initio*. Although the question of whether SAP has been a blessing or a curse to African development is still a subject of controversy in some respects, the position is that it made a nonsense of the Africans and did considerable damage to the socio-economic existence of the people. The standard of living of the people plummeted as currencies were devalued, jobs trimmed, careers destroyed, public utilities privatized/commercialized, local industries exposed vulnerably, governments became irresponsibly insensitive and corruption skyrocketed.

Rural economies were assaulted and robbed as agriculture lost its value and commodity farmers were pauperized. Largely, SAP as adopted in sub-Saharan Africa, particularly West Africa, damaged state confidence and sovereignty, and compromised material and non-material wellbeing of the majority of Africans. Foreign institutions and personalities in form of 'experts' dominated local experts, institutions and policy environments, which had negative implications for national psyche and national security. These situations led to national/regional/continental priority misplacements as Bretton Woods organizations bombarded nations in the region with stringent conditionality. In Nigeria, for instance, the SAP era is fondly remembered for dangerous individualism, erosion of social solidity, increased conflicts engendered by survival struggles, high crime rates, annihilated middle class, compromised education system, unprecedentedly high corruption rate and ground-breaking ineffective austerity measures. The extremely high corruption, for example, introduced the notion and ascendancy of the 'national cake' into the Nigerian socio-political lexicon.

The political economy of SAP in Africa is certainly more of negativity in terms of outcomes, and the impact of SAP will surely be felt in the history, present and future of West African development, particularly as the variants of the policy are still being implemented in various guises of reforms in the region. Nations appear to have been fixated at some point in the dictates of SAP. The nauseating economic and general development consequences of SAP in Africa since the 1980s has particularly had negative implications on West Africa's development and it frequently makes them forgo long-term development frameworks for short-term ones and this includes ECOWAS regional integration plans. Member states thus give more commitment to national exigencies and nation building to built credibility, especially in democratic settings, as this could determine perceptions of government performance and future election outcomes. The orientation is thus a battle for relative socioeconomic stability in the short term at home, no matter how it is achieved. Sustainable development is certainly elusive in West Africa today. And underdevelopment is obviously extensive from the foregoing regardless of where you draw the line between development and underdevelopment.

It is therefore important for ECOWAS to pay deserved attention to development problems in the region if it is to achieve its objectives especially as no state in the region has significantly changed positively in terms of development. The development models adopted in the region, including SAP, were based on Modernization Theory. Those models were/are bound to fail as no two societies can entirely develop the same way, given the unique socio-cultural and politico-economic dynamics prevalent of individual societies. This is more so when the societies of reference are in different socio-geographic domains like Asia/Europe/America and Africa. For instance, it would be impossible to reproduce in West Africa the elements that jump-started South Korean and Taiwanese development, as the rich foreign economies that sustained their aggressive export activities no longer subsist.

Development frameworks adopted in the region hitherto were based on the incorporation of less developed nations of Africa prematurely into the world capitalist system in a manner that makes the Africans subservient and dependent on the developed nations of the North (Olutayo, Olutayo and Omobowale 2008). Such relationships are certain to underdevelop African nations further as the developed ones exploit the imbalance to develop themselves even more in the face of challenging development environments globally since all nations are, in the final analysis, still developing. This is why, for dependency theorists, the development of African nations is impossible, except such relationships are critically re-assessed against present objective realities. It is also against these realities that Meilink (2003) concluded that evidently that was why the theoretical framework of the IMF in marshalling SAP in Africa was inadequate.

The Necessities of Harmonized Alternative Development Approach in West Africa

The drive globally in contemporary terms is for regions to coordinate state activities to galvanize common fronts that could ensure development. This is usually all-inclusive to ensure comprehensive human development in the region in the face of irreversible globalization and global market competition that could compromise weak nations' development. The ECOWAS region is certainly no exception and must guarantee a harmonized or near-harmonized development approach, especially as an alternative to failed SAP ones that were imposed on West Africa since the 1980s. Ameliorating and challenging SAP was particularly difficult for ECOWAS as the regional organization was just stabilizing after its formation just about a decade earlier. Now, however, ECOWAS has stabilized and should be consolidating with workable development approaches in the region. It is, however, important to note that harmonized alternative efforts are not entirely new in Africa. But experience suggests that such alternative development paradigms are frequently rejected by governments and political elites in the region.

International institutions and African political elites rejected such proposals and under-played their critical roles in African development, while they imposed foreign ones on them as was the case in the era of SAP. In fact, there have been protracted debates between African intellectuals and the foreign 'experts' at the Bretton Woods institutions since 1976 over the best approach in the continent but the Bretton Woods institutions have always triumphed over the African intellectuals. Cases in point are those of the Lagos Plan of Action and the African Alternative Frameworks to Structural Adjustment Programme for Socio-Economic Recovery and Transformation (AAF-SAP). Although the documents were excellent in predicting the negative implications of SAP and economic globalization, they were not adopted and implemented by African governments regardless of the efforts of the African intellectuals. Rather than listen to the alternatives, governments agreed with foreign institutions that usually trace underdevelopment to poor local policies rather than external forces.

An example of such official rejection was in the 1981 by the World Bank through the popular Berg Report (Towards Accelerated Development in sub-Saharan Africa) which characteristically blamed local factors for sub-Saharan Africa's underdevelopment and recommended a return to outward-oriented programme of export of raw materials, rolling back states' intervention and freeing up market forces. Generally, the Berg Report of the World Bank upheld and encouraged the Bank's support for SAP and export-led development approach. It is therefore important to note that the challenge is not that intellectuals who have not suggested viable alternative development approach(es) but that of African governments and their foreign expert partners have refused to accept and adopt the alternative development strategies. African governments lack commitment to alternatives. In fact they appear to be averse to them. They have refused to commit time, finances and political resources to such approaches. The orthodoxy of the Bretton Woods institutions regarding development approaches in Africa is understandable. The Bretton Woods institutions finance the adoption of development approaches and experimentations while African political elites receive the funds and implement the prescriptions even to the detriment of the common good.

And, why should the North as represented by the Bretton Woods institutions finance African alternative approaches – approaches that negate and often counteract the Northern Agenda? It is unlikely and certainly irrational! Governance in Africa is thus an important element in the alternative development agenda issue. Where is the commitment of the African leaders to the alternative approaches? Asians were/are committed; Latin Americans were/are committed and they are reaping the benefits as some are now even ahead of some European nations on the development scale. They have become the twentieth and twenty-first century' development tigers, dragons and miracles! How have even the alternatives been managed over time by African social scientists who are/were in government? These are strategic issues that must be addressed objectively by ECOWAS and the African development community. There is the need to encourage governments of member states to be responsible to the alternative approaches on development. There is also the need for the African governments and political elites to appreciate local experts and their outputs in the region. And there is the need for the local intellectuals to be committed to the implementation of alternative approaches at every given opportunity.

The time to act is now. West African states today are emerging stronger and more promising as a few like Nigeria and Togo are now ranked amongst the best emerging economies in the world. The need to build on these positive development indicators is rife and the needed approach is a return to the state especially as they are now emerging stronger than the pre-SAP and SAP eras. There must be regulation. And the states, through their governments, should regulate activities of nations and not blindly deregulate. Regulation is the primary activity and essence of governments. Economically, the primary step to development is to grow the Gross Domestic Product (GDP) and the second is employment. It is impossible to create wealth and development by unemployment and inflation and, above all, inflation creates poverty and poverty is underdevelopment. These are what deregulation and rolling back the state have created in the West African states. It is a strong state and viable government that can successfully manage these complex situations in Africa today through regulation.

Rolling back the state cannot successfully manage these complexities in Africa for the future. African states need to decidedly unleash the energy of their people for efficient capacity utilization for development. Nigeria and Venezuela case are both members of Organization of Petroleum Exporting Countries (OPEC) but Nigeria is rolling back the state while Venezuela is 'rolling in' the state. At present, the local price of petrol (Premium Motor Spirit [PMS]) is 16 times higher in Nigeria than Venezuela and Nigeria is the only country in OPEC that imports petroleum. Rolling back the state is not the solution to Africa's development debacle and it is not surprising that such policies have failed since the 1980s. In the Nigerian oil sector, for instance, Nigeria has rolled back the state 17 times and this has failed 17 times beginning from 1 October 1978 at the wake of the global oil crisis that ushered in SAP. The warning therefore is that it is time to return to state as African states lack the capacity to compete effectively in the delicate global systems. Interestingly, Nigeria recently faced this stark reality in its banking and aviation industries, for example. The two sensitive and strategic industries were to crash heavily of recent and the Central Bank of Nigeria had to release billions of Naira (millions of US dollars) as bailout funds. A similar bailout fund is now also being lobbied for to shore up the downstream petroleum sector of the economy as it is also at the verge of collapse.

All African states must invest in their intellectuals to generate contemporary and competitive ideological knowledge that can continually provide alternative sustainable development approaches. This is development that is friendly today and protective tomorrow. This will include environment, gender, age, technology and health sustainability? and not just the economy. Unfortunately, intellectual and ideological investments are not particularly appreciated in Africa. Attention to education in sub-Saharan Africa today is disproportionately on science and technology while disciplines that engage socio-cultural, psychological and ideological dynamics of development are least valued. In Nigeria, two governments have recently attempted to scrap such courses from the Nigerian university curricular. These were the Abacha's regime and the Obasanjo government – one – military and the other a democratic! What stopped Abacha was his sudden death, while the needed time and democratic due diligence prevented Obasanjo. Chief Olusegun Obasanjo's government advocated for the scrapping of courses like Philosophy from the universities because, according to him, why study such courses when you know no one will employ you with such certificates.

That was and is the attitude of the African political elites. One of the foremost private universities in Nigeria today is owned by the ex-president, Chief Olusegun Obasanjo. It is a purely science and technology institution. Africa needs to build and re-build its extensive knowledge infrastructure, if the continent will develop in real terms. Comprehensive ideas rule the world and generate development. It is heresy that only by science and technology knowledge and entrepreneurship skills can the African continent develop. This is a dangerous idea and should be jettisoned in its entirety. This should be discouraged because it is grossly misleading and dangerous. Government policies in the continent on economic reconstruction, technological diffusion and innovations, engineering and business development must be all-inclusive and consistent. These must be married with Social Sciences, Arts, Humanities, Administration and Agriculture and collapsed with regional integration if they are to really benefit ECOWAS nations particularly.

Unaccountable leadership, poor political elites' capacities and widespread corruption are also development challenges in the sub-region. Thus, in harmonizing the alternative development approaches, governance environments must be improved on the continent. It is only within these trajectories that the strategic opportunities in the harmonized alternative approach(es) to development in the region could be productive. It is also necessary to appropriate the knowledge and capacities of the Africans in the diaspora. This is very important as Africans in the diaspora have traversed the two divides of the worlds and have experienced the two policy domains. They therefore have the capacity to appreciate the two policy domains and contribute positively to the alternative policy formulation and adoption for sustainable development in the region, rather than relying on foreign experts that have no stake in the African development process.

Reflections on the Alternative Approach: Statements of Conclusion

African nations must develop, and the development must be sustainable. More importantly too, the sustainable development must start now. To start now and to be sustainable, however, the continent must evolve an alternative development approach. Particularly, West African nations' age-long development problems suggest the need to rethink and retool the development strategies adopted hitherto. Development approaches adopted by African nations since the 1980s have done nothing but make development in the region a mirage and make African leaders and finance ministers international beggars (Boafo-Arthur 2003). The first stage in African development is thus a return to the state. According to Boafo-Arthur (2003:48):

> It has become fashionable for some analysts to ignore the fact that the vaunted phenomena economic development of the East Asian Tigers was attained by strong and capable states – not by states that were solely at the mercy of uncontrolled external phenomena often manipulated by the West to suit their developmental needs. So long as this situation persists (erosion of state power), Africa's ability to wiggle itself out of its developmental quagmire is a matter of conjecture.

The return of state power is thus a must for Africa's development. There is no such a thing as a completely liberalized economy. While the United States of America (USA) used to be a fair example of a liberalized economy, the recent global financial crisis, also known as the global economic meltdown, has even proved otherwise. In this instance, the American government had to intervene in the economic system to save the state from total collapse and this was/is the practice across the world. Aside the Lagos Plan of Action of 1980 and the AAF-SAP of 1989, as the two major alternative policy in the African development stable, some contemporary African intellectuals have contributed to the subject. Examples of these indigenous intellectuals are: Olutayo, Olutayo and Omobowale (2005), Boafo-Arthur (2003) and Ake (1996). Olutayo, Olutayo and Omobowale's (2005) alternative focused on return to the Lagos Plan of Action and the AAF-SAP framework but with the establishment of independent grassroots organizations at various levels (p. 246). For Olutayo, Olutayo and Omobowale (2005), these grassroots organizations are to be voluntary, democratically operated and enshrined in the people's culture – to appropriate culture and tradition for self-realization. The Olutayo, Olutayo and Omobowale (2005) alternative is deployment of LPA and AAF-SAP with social capital appropriation.

For Boafo-Arthur (2003), the alternative is the return of the state to the economy. According to Boafo-Arthur (2003), serious attention must be given to the operation of a mixed economy. This mixed economy suggested by Boafo-Arthur (2003) must be summarily blended with African leaders' political will. An important point of convergence between the Olutayo, Olutayo and Omobowale (2005) alternative and the Boafo-Arthur (2003) alternative is the appreciation of the LPA and the AAF-SAP framework. But while Olutayo, Olutayo and Omobowale (2005) included social capital appropriation, Boafo-Arthur (2003) emphasized return to the state principally. While Ake (1996) also appreciated the LPA and the AAF-SAP framework, he suggested a populist alternative based on marshalling the energy of ordinary people, otherwise known as community mobilization. This is through smallholder agriculture underwritten by popular democracy and participation to increase efficiency and productivity of small farmers and rural industries.

Ake's (1996) alternative thus rests on the tripod of the market, the state and the community. A closer look at the Olutayo, Olutayo and Omobowale (2005) and the Ake (1996) alternatives thus reveals another point of convergence through the community engagements. We suggest a return to the LPA and AAF-SAP fundamentally because these policies are realistic, objective, comprehensive, pragmatic, endogenous, compliant and intellectually rigorous. Contemporary African development strategy must also return to the state. Although survival necessities are making some African states appropriate state powers, coordinated efforts must be made in the region to comprehensively return to the state. Development drives in the region must move from rolling back the state to 'rolling in' the state. It is only through the state that development in Africa can be realized, especially within the context of weak isolated economies in the region in the face of intimidating and sometimes corrosive globalization.

Hence, African development must be sustainable and inclusive. In other words, against deep-rooted patriarchy in Africa, the development alternative being suggested in this paper includes women and makes the development approach gender-compliant. This strategy is community-based and participatory to include people at the grassroots. It is not a detached development effort. At the same time, external influence or origin should be minimized. This encourages local development innovations that are workable within peculiar situations devoid of external ulterior motives. This is why strong states are expressly needed and must be returned to in the African states' development puzzle. Development policies and strategy as have been proposed in this chapter appreciate the need for the environment. The environment is a major component of this strategy. The environment (physical, natural and socio-cultural) must be respected and protected.

The environment must not be degraded through development activities and policies. The land must not be degraded; the water must be protected; forests must be conserved; climate must be reckoned with while the socio-cultural infrastructure must be conserved and deployed regularly for development. This is the historical, socio-cultural, political, economic, global and physical ecologies integration alternative development approach. It is an alternative factor in the appreciation of the consequences of complex intermingling of natural existences, external forces, regional elements, national exigencies, and the community level imperatives in African development.

References

Ake, C., 1996, *Democracy and Development in Africa,* Washington DC, Brookings Institution.

Ayadi, O.F., Adegbite, E.O., and Ayadi, E.S., 2008, 'Structural Adjustment, Financial Sector Development and Economic Prosperity in Nigeria', *International Journal of Finance and Economics,* Issue 15, pp. 318-331.

Boafo-Arthur, K., 2003, 'Tackling Africa's Developmental Dilemmas: Is Globalization the Answer?' *Journal of Third World Studies,* XX, No.1, pp. 25-54.

Ibeabuchi, S.N., Essien, S.N., Appah, E.E., and Idowu, A.E., 2003, 'Liberalization and Privatization of Public Utilities in Nigeria', in O.J. Nnana, S.O. Alade, and F.O. Odoko, *Contemporary Economic Policy Issues in Nigeria,* Nigeria, Central Bank of Nigeria (CBN), pp. 56-102.

Juma, C., 2006, *Redesigning African Economies: The Role of Engineering in International Development* 2006 Hilton Lecture, The Royal Academy of Engineering.

Meilink, H., 2003, *Structural Adjustment Programmes on the African Continent: The Theoretical Foundations of IMF/World Bank Reform Policies.* ASC Working Paper No. 53. December.

Olutayo, A.O. and Omobowale, A.O., 2003, 'Globalization, Democracy and the New Partnership for Africa's Development (NEPAD)', *African Journal of the Psychological Study of Social Issues,* 8.2, pp. 228-242.

Olutayo, A.O. Olutayo, M.A.O. and Omobowale, A.O., 2005, 'TINA, aids and the underdevelopment in Africa', *Brazilian Journal of Political Economy,* 28. 2, pp. 239-248, April-June.

Taylor, K.S., 2001, *Human Society and the Global Economy.* Atomicdogpublishing.com. http://distance-ed.bcc.ctc.edu/econ100/ksttext/underdev/catchup.thm. Accessed 10 March 2008.

10

Policing Irregular Migration in the West African Sub-region: Implications for Regional Integration

Ikuteyijo Lanre Olusegun

Introduction

The need for regional integration is borne out of a number of factors ranging from economic advancement to guaranteeing human rights and security. In the age of globalization, most countries embarked upon regional integration schemes in the belief that larger economic units would be better able to compete and participate in the world economy. However, some of the emergent policies on regional integration are faced with challenges in the new world order. Prominent among them is the effective management of migration of people across the sub-region as well as monitoring the activities of organized criminal networks operating along the borders. In the West African sub-region, the need for effective policing and regional cooperation is necessitated by the emergent economic and political challenges faced by countries in the sub-region. The aftermath of the Arab Springs presented some security challenges to the West African sub-region. This manifested in the proliferation of small arms and light weapons with attendant rise in the rate of armed robbery, insurgencies and terrorism. Armed resistance in Mali resulting from the activities of the radical Islamist Tuareg groups, is almost plunging the country into a civil war. In Nigeria, not long after the insurrection caused by the Niger Delta militants had been doused by the Amnesty Programme of the government, there are crises with Islamic terrorists from the northern parts. This group known as Boko Haram, is reputed to have links with terrorist groups outside the country like the Al Qaeda and Shabab. Reports have it that most of the trainings of the terrorists groups were held outside the country. Criminal activities involving pirates, kidnapping, human trafficking of especially women and children, drug peddling, illegal importation of goods, armed robbery, advanced fee fraud (also known as "419") and other trans-national criminal networks are emerging from different parts of the sub-region. The borders across the sub-region tend to get more porous as most of these crimes are usually perpetrated despite several efforts to curb them. All these imply that there is the need to step up inter-country cooperation in form of information and intelligence sharing as far as migration management is concerned. This chapter therefore examines the implications of policing these challenges, which no doubt are fuelled by the changing migration configurations in the sub-region on the much needed regional integration. Other specific objectives of this chapter are to:

1. Analyse the challenges posed by irregular migration to the regional integration of the West African sub-region;
2. Discuss the various types of trans-border crimes in the sub-region with a view to understanding the role of irregular migration;
3. Examine the need for effective policing of aftermaths of changing migration configurations in the West African sub-region;
4. Assess the implications of the ECOWAS borderless pact for regional integration in the sub-region;
5. Discuss the implications of political instability and rising insurgences on the regional integration of the sub-region; and
6. Suggest appropriate strategies for harnessing the gains of regional integration through proactively addressing the challenges.

Irregular Migration: Conceptual Clarifications

A number of definitions and modifications have been made over the years to what is to be described as irregular migration, with arguments and counter arguments as to why certain words could not be adequate to describe the phenomenon. Over the years, the phenomenon of irregular migration has been described by various scholars using different labels (Portes 1978; de Genova 2002; Espenshade 1995; Guild 2004; Baldwin-Edwards 2008; Triandafyllidou 2010; Cvajner and Sciortino 2010; Donato and Armenta 2011; Kubal 2012). Some of these labels include 'illegal migration', 'undocumented migration', 'unauthorized migration', and 'clandestine migration' among others. The various conceptual debates arose following different political and ideological viewpoints in conceiving these concepts. For instance, Koser (2005) criticized the use of 'illegal' to qualify migrants for the following reasons. First, the term 'illegal' connotes criminality and most irregular migrants are not criminals. This was corroborated by the UN Special Rapporteur on the Rights of Non-Citizens, which recommended that countries of destination should not treat immigrants (even those without valid documents) as criminals. Second, since irregular migrants are humans with Fundamental Human Rights, irrespective of their status, defining them as illegal will therefore amount to denying their humanity (Guild 2010).

Methodologically, however, considering the fact that irregular migrants constitute a hard-to-reach population given their invisible nature, the subjects of most studies on irregular migration have been those who left the country without valid documents, mainly through human smuggling and trafficking, as well as undocumented migrants trapped in the criminal justice systems of receiving countries. Incidentally, there seem not to be an end to the 'definition dilemma' as what constitutes irregular migration has continued to be the subject of controversy among legal and migration scholars. In the context of this chapter, irregular migration means the entering of a country's border without the possession of valid documents or the act of entering a country in violation of the migration norms of such country (De Haas 2007; Adepoju 2006). Notably, migrants with irregular status may include those who are in the destination countries in search of asylum or who have been displaced from their places of origin. Hence, for the purpose of this chapter, asylum seekers and refugees, who are denied entry and those who have either entered the countries of destination in violation of the norms of migration or those who entered legally but have overstayed their visas, are all categorized as irregular migrants. Amnesty International (2010) reported that in some countries, asylum seekers and other irregular migrants are treated the same way. Since this chapter addresses the issue of migration within the sub-region, the definition of irregular migrants will be those who contravene the ECOWAS Protocol on Free Movement. The law only allows citizens of ECOWAS member states to travel to any of the member states without a visa for an upward of 90 days. However, various studies have emerged to suggest that the free movement pact is responsible for the proliferation of human trafficking across the sub-region (Ehindero and Idemudia 2006).

Responses to Irregular Migration

The growing number of people who are involved in migration worldwide has made migration management a complex issue for managers, and, has become a real challenge to maintaining a satisfactory migration policy that could respond to all interests (Ikuteyijo 2013). On the global level, migration management continues to pose many challenges to different countries as people continue to move at the fastest rate recorded in human history. According to the United Nations, over 180 million people live outside their places of origin worldwide and this has its consequences. One such consequence is the increasing need for migration managers to be more scientific in their approach; unlike what obtained in the past, where the issue of human rights was relegated to the background. The International Organization for Migration (IOM) estimated that there were over 500,000 irregular migrants in the European Union (Stan 2006); and by the end of the 20th century, all developed nations had become countries of immigration (Massey 2003).

The increasing trend of irregular migration has presented many challenges in diverse ways to many countries, especially countries of destination. Arising from this increasing trend as well as the need to minimize the adverse consequences of irregular migration, countries of origin, transit and destination have engaged in constructive dialogues at international, regional, sub-regional and national levels to ensure that the benefits of migration are realized while the dangers are minimized. Adepoju and Van der Wiel (2010) have, however, noted that this awakening has resulted in new initiatives and the adoption of common strategic frameworks and migration policies at all levels -- national, sub-regional and regional.

About half a century ago, many countries in West Africa unilaterally used mass expulsion as the major policy of managing migration. These policies of mass deportation and expulsion were actually aimed at specific nationals, who were 'labelled' as irregular migrants. At this period, migrants were used as scapegoats in the event of economic downturn and they were blamed for increasing rates of crime. Thus their expulsions were carried out under such excuses (Adepoju 2006). Adepoju (2005) captured some specific cases as follows:

1. In 1958, Ivory Coast expelled over 1,000 Benin and Togo nationals, while in the same year Chad expelled thousands of Benin nationals who were described as 'illegal migrants'.
2. In 1964, Ivory Coast expelled about 16,000 Beninese, while in 1968 Ghanaian fishermen were expelled from Sierra-Leone, Guinea and Ivory Coast.
3. On December 1969, Ghana expelled all 'illegal aliens' without a valid residence permit and this exercise involved about half a million people mostly from Nigeria, Upper Volta and Niger.
4. In 1983 and 1985, there were mass expulsions of undocumented or irregular migrants from Nigeria. These migrants were accused of engaging in illegal activities such as begging and prostitution, besides not having legal migration documents. (Ikuteyijo 2013)

Unfortunately, the issue is not too different although there is growing awareness among various nations of the world on the need to manage migration, not unilaterally but in conjunction with identified countries of transit and destination (Ghosh 2000). For instance, in Nigeria, the attempt to manage the problem of irregular migration, especially that of human trafficking and child labour, was carried out in conjunction with countries like Italy and Spain (identified countries of destination) and the policies made were more bilateral or multilateral in nature as the case may be. Libya also enjoyed the support of some EU countries like Spain and Italy as a result of the realization of the fact that Libya had become a major transit country for migrants. In fact, a former Libyan leader (Ghaddafi) was once reported to have demanded a certain amount of money from the EU to help fight the problem of irregular migration. However, at the sub-regional level, response to irregular migration is mainly defined by the ECOWAS Protocol on Free Movement, which unfortunately has not been adhered to by countries of destination in times of political crises and economic hardship. There is still an urgent need for migration managers in the sub-region to respect the human rights of migrants who pass through their borders. The idea of 'sacrificing' irregular migrants in times of economic hardship should cease and this can only be achieved when there is a formal forum to discuss migration management in the sub-region. Hence, Adepoju (2005) advocated a West African Dialogue on Migration Management for all stakeholders, where the media general public would be enlightened in order to avoid the misrepresentations, ignorance and xenophobia that currently characterize response to irregular migration.

Trans-border Crimes as a Challenge to Regional Integration

The regulation of activities across the borders of West African states is an essential factor in ensuring peace and stability as well as promoting the necessary political and socio-economic activities needed for regional integration in the sub-region. Inevitably, migration forms an essential part of these trans-border activities as people and goods often move from one country to another. The founding fathers of ECOWAS had, in their wisdom and in response to the need to facilitate free movement of goods and personnel across the sub-region, formulated the Protocol on Free Movement of persons, which was to pave way for economic integration in the ECOWAS community. However, the management of most borders in West Africa can best be described as shoddy and inadequate. This stems from both structural and human factors. Structurally, West African border control lacks the technical infrastructure and human resources needed to protect the borders. Likewise, the dilapidation of border control points is compounded by the dispiritedness of the security services personnel. They are generally poorly paid and feel isolated or unmotivated, without proper working tools or proper protection, for example, against attacks by criminals and cross-border traffickers (Fall 2005). This is evident in the inability of the Nigerian Immigration Service to stem/arrest the influx of Niger and other non-Nigerians involved in the Boko Haram insurgency which has embroiled the country for a while (Ikuteyijo 2013).

Addo (2006) attempted a categorization of trans-border crimes in the sub-region as presented in Table 1.

Table 1: Classification of Trans-Border Crimes in West Africa

Predominant Border Crimes	Country/Zones of activity	Groups/Actors involved	Transit states	Recipient states
Narcotics/drug trafficking	Cape Verde, Ghana, Nigeria, Togo	Narcotics/drug dealers	Ghana, Togo, Benin, Nigeria	Spain, Portugal, U.S.A., South Africa
Internet Crime (Advance fee fraud/money Laundering)	Nigeria, Ghana, Cote D'Ivoire, Sierra Leone	Advance fee fraud gangs or syndicates/wealthy business men or government officials	Syndicates commute from Western parts of West Africa (Senegal) across to the Eastern parts (Benin/Nigeria)	Nigeria and other countries where 419 fraudsters are resident
Human trafficking	All across West Africa but mainly around Benin/Nigeria and Cote D'Ivoire/Burkina Faso	Traffickers who serve sometimes as middlemen, trade and business partners	Mainly Ghana and Sierra Leone	Other West African countries, North America and Middle East
Firearms Trafficking	Ghana/Togo/Benin /Nigeria/Sierra Leone/Liberia/Guin ea/ Cote D'Ivoire,	Rebels/local manufacturers of firearms and middlemen	Togo/Benin/G uinea Bissau and Gambia	Nigeria/Liberia/ Guinea/Sierra Leone/ Cote D'Ivoire,

Trans-border crimes in the sub-region could be discussed as follows:

Human Trafficking and Child Labour in the West African Sub-region

Human trafficking is the second highest world crime after illegal arms transactions. It has also been described as the modern form of human slavery which, like the old form, involves the trading of humans as commodities with no regard for their fundamental human rights. The United Nations estimates that 2.5 million people are in forced labour (including sexual exploitation) at any time as a result of trafficking (International Labour Organization [ILO] 2007; Goldin *et al* 2011). There are two main types of trafficking: internal and international trafficking. While internal trafficking takes place within the borders of a country, international trafficking involves movement of victims across national borders.

The human and economic costs of human trafficking are enormous on individuals and communities. According to conservative estimates, the cost of trafficking in terms of underpayment of wages and recruitment fees is over $20 billion (ILO 2009:2; World Bank 2010:1). Besides the economic costs, it also involves criminality and human rights implications. The most publicised aspects of human trafficking are sex trafficking and child labour. Children are also being incorporated into the sex tourism industry. The United Nations' Children Emergency Funds estimated that about 1.2 million children are trafficked each year (UNICEF 2003). The victims of trafficking (mostly women and children) are often either kidnapped or lured from their home by traffickers under various guises like securing employment or pursuing educational advancement (UNODC 2009; Goldin *et al* 2011).

The involvement of African countries in the global human trafficking network is raising serious concerns as most African countries constitute one or more of source, transit and destination countries for trafficked victims. In the Horn of Africa, human trafficking is exacerbated by the natural and human induced catastrophes that have threatened peace and stability in the region (Manian 2010:13). Victims of human trafficking in the region often undergo dual victimization arising from the conflict in the environment as well as the exploitation of their bodies and human rights.

Lastly, in southern Africa, human trafficking is rampant in three main countries, namely: South Africa, Mozambique and Zimbabwe. Human trafficking is thriving in South Africa as a result of: poverty, child and female oppression, limited border security and sexual myths. In southern Africa, human trafficking takes various forms including sexual exploitation, forced labour, slavery and domestic servitude (World Bank 2010). The National Prosecution Authority of South Africa (2010:iv) identified four major streams of human trafficking flows in South Africa which are: trafficking to South Africa from outside Africa; trafficking to South Africa from within Africa; trafficking within the national borders of South Africa; and trafficking that uses South Africa as a transit point to other countries. In West Africa, Nigeria, Ghana and Senegal have been identified as source, transit, and destination countries for trafficked women and children (Adepoju 2005:92). There is an established network of traffickers who run the business around the West African hub. The major source/

origin countries for child labour are Nigeria, Mali, Burkina Faso, Mauritania and Togo, while the major countries of origin for prostitution are Nigeria and Togo (Anarfi 1998; Adepoju 2005:78). Apart from the hubs within the sub-region, traffickers also 'export' children and young women to some countries in Europe and the Gulf States (Taylor 2002; ILO 2003; Human Rights Watch 2003; De Haas 2008:32). In fact, De Haas (2008) noted that out of the 27,000 migrants apprehended by Moroccan police in 2004, over half were of West African origin, with most migrants coming from the Gambia, Ghana, Mali, and Senegal, respectively. Human trafficking in East Africa is dominated by Uganda and Kenya as source and transit countries for women working as prostitutes in the Gulf States (Adepoju 2005:78). There are established syndicates run by foreign businessmen, who specialise in trafficking young girls to Europe. Edo and Delta States in Nigeria are particularly notorious for the trafficking of young females for the purpose of sexual slavery in Europe and even in some other parts of the continent. Available evidence shows that there are established syndicates that are usually organized across countries, especially in the West African sub-region (Adepoju 2005; Ikuteyijo 2013).

Proliferation of Small Arms

Another trans-border crime in the West African sub-region is the proliferation of small arms and light weapons (SALW). Darkwa (2011:13) identified three main sources of SALW within the West African sub-region namely: 'extant stocks that are recycled; new imports, which may include brand-new weapons and ammunition as well as used weapons recycled from outside the sub-region; and local craft production in countries of the sub-region'. Over the years in different countries in the sub-region, where there have been insurrections against the government, the use of SALW have been prominent and this likewise helped in sustaining the proliferation. Incidentally, attempts by both ECOWAS and the United Nations to restore peace to some of the troubled zones inadvertently led to the further proliferation of SALW. Some scholars have submitted that soldiers on peacekeeping missions became active agents in the circulation of SALW. While some soldiers were rounded up and disarmed by insurgent groups like RUF, others deliberately sold their weapons in exchange for survival in the battle field (Leighton 2000; Berman 2001; Darkwa 2011).

The circulation of SALW is exacerbated by the porous nature and inadequate management of most of the borders in the sub-region. Addo (2006) noted that the porous borders engender cross-border crime and instability in the sub-region due to the lack of an appropriate mechanism for monitoring movement and illegal activities across borders. For instance, Nigeria, one of the most prominent countries in the sub-region, has 770 kilometres of shared land border with the Republic of Benin; about 1,500 kilometres with the Republic of the Niger; 1,700 kilometres with Cameroon; and 90 kilometres with Chad. This is different from the 850 kilometres of maritime border which the country has with the Atlantic Ocean (Yacubu 2005). Naturally, it is a big challenge to adequately man all these borders, as the country's immigration service does not have the staff strength needed to do that. Besides size of borders, some countries in the sub-region find it difficult to finance border security; hence their borders have become hotspots for organized criminal gangs. For instance, the security officials of Mali and Senegal worked for months without payment because of the states' inability to fund the joint patrol of their borders (Ndime 2005). Scholars have identified some factors that encourage the proliferation of arms and ammunition. These include, *inter alia*, the rise of ethnic militarism, religious crises, inter-tribal conflicts, insurrection and terrorism, and political violence (Yacubu 2005). Moreover, small arms are ubiquitous in that they are cheap, easy to transport and conceal, simple to maintain and easy to handle.

In an attempt to curb the circulation of illicit weapons in the sub-region, ECOWAS has made a number of efforts. For example, in 1998, ECOWAS member states adopted a Declaration of the Moratorium on the Importation, Exportation, and Manufacture of Light Weapons in Abuja (Addo 2006). Likewise in 2006, the ECOWAS Small Arms Control Programme (ECOSAP) was established to build the capacities of member states in combating the proliferation and illegal circulation of small arms in West Africa (ECOSAP Webpage, cited in Darkwa 2011). However, some of the challenges facing the actualization of the laudable goals of these policies are numerous. One of these is the lack of institutional capacity to train security sector personnel and law enforcement agencies on the mechanisms for addressing small arms proliferation (ECOSAP Annual Report 2010; Darkwa 2011). Another challenge is that ECOWAS member states lack the technological equipment needed to combat such proliferation in the sub-region. For example, metal detectors are either absent or in short supply at points of entry into several countries in West Africa. Furthermore, several airports as well as seaports in the sub-region lack scanners, which are essential for the detection of contraband goods, including weapons concealed in luggage. This shortage of equipment is compounded by the lack of spare parts and; supporting infrastructure, and the dependence on external sources of supply. Lastly, the porous nature of most borders in the sub-region coupled with official corruption among customs and immigration officials make it easy for smugglers to circulate SALW in the sub-region.

Political Instability and Terrorism as Threats to Regional Integration

It is common knowledge that many countries in West Africa are vulnerable to terrorist operations. Poor governance is linked to terrorism because in the absence of good governance, corruption, organized crime and poverty proliferate (Trosper 2009). The West African sub-region is constituted by countries which have had their fair share in terms of political instability. Out of the sixteen countries that make up ECOWAS, only Cape Verde has not had a military putsch. From 1962 to 2003, the other fifteen states in the sub-region have had military coup d'états. Successive governments have always accused their predecessors of gross financial misappropriation and administrative indiscipline. The clamour for the control of resources has bred all forms of misgivings among various segments (usually along ethnic and religious lines) who believe they have been short-changed. One of the indications of the threats of terrorism and political instability in the sub-region is the outbreak and consequences of civil wars in Liberia, Sierra Leone, Guinea Bissau and Côte d'Ivoire; the Tuareg revolts in Niger and Mali; and the insurgency in Nigeria's Niger Delta and some of the states in the north. In Nigeria, for example, the Niger Delta was engulfed in crises for some time due to what some observers described as marginalization and environmental degradation. It took the insurgencies of some militant groups to attract the attention of the government to the plight of the residents. The militias who employed the use of sophisticated weapons, which in some cases outmatched the fire power of the country's security forces, resorted to kidnapping of oil workers and sabotage of oil pipelines as well as illegal oil bunkering. Apparently, what began as an agitation for the equitable distribution of the oil wealth of the Niger Delta, snowballed into a criminal dimension (Darkwa 2011). Nigeria's economy was the worst hit at the peak of the crises as the insurgency caused the country almost 30% loss of her daily production and expected oil revenues. Not long after the Niger Delta crises had subsided and political power shifted from the north to the south, the northern part of the country also took over the baton of insurrection as some groups accused the ruling government of discrimination and launched attacks on government installations as well as non-indigenes, especially members of other religions. The inglorious Boko Haram group, which initially began with campaigns against western education, was hijacked by politicians and the nation is yet to recover from the rubble.

Apparently, insurgencies across the West African sub-region, coupled with the porous borders and limited resources to control them, provide an opportunity for terrorist groups to expand their communication and training and to export their terrorist schemes, thereby increasing regional instability. Investigations have shown that there were links between the Boko Haram and the Al Qaeda group in the Maghreb as some car bombs detonated by Boko Haram militants in the aftermaths of the UN House bombing bore signature elements of the improvised explosives used by the Qaeda offshoot in the Sahel. The forensic evidence shows that the group may have shared its tactics and techniques with the Nigerian terrorist organization. Furthermore, there were reports that the war in Mali is affecting the operations of some of these terrorist groups, prominent among which are the Boko Haram. In Mali, many of the Tuaregs currently fighting in the rebellion were reported to have received training from the late Gadhafi's Islamic Legion during his tenure in Libya. Therefore many of the combatants are experienced with a variety of warfare techniques that have posed major problems to the national governments of Mali and Niger.

The scattered evidence support the need for an effective monitoring of the borders in the sub-region. This could involve the coordinated training of border managers in order to increase the professionalization, enhance interagency communication and expand the capacity of the police and other security agencies to more effectively prevent and respond to terrorist attacks. Furthermore, countries in the sub-region should enact legislations to deal with the recent development of terrorism and not rely on some of their criminal laws, which are apparently inadequate to address the new trend of crime.

ECOWAS Borderless Pact and Implications for Regional Integration

In order to actualize the ECOWAS borderless pact whose main objective is to facilitate the free movement of citizens of member states across the sub-region, the heads of state of ECOWAS member countries at a meeting in Abuja, Nigeria in March 2000 agreed to create a borderless sub-region after the mode of the Schengen pact. It was also agreed at the meeting that rigid border formulations would be eliminated and the use of passport scanning machines would be introduced as part of border procedures. Furthermore, the numerous roadblocks and security checkpoints on highways across countries were to be dismantled to avoid delays and extortion of passengers. In the area of security, there were to be joint border patrols involving neighbouring countries like Nigeria, Niger, Benin, Togo, Ghana, Mali and Burkina Faso. There was to be a closer working relationship between police and internal security agencies in terms of the exchange of ideas and intelligence sharing. All these were to be precluded by intensive advocacy in terms of awareness campaign among immigration and customs officials in the affected states (Adepoju 2005). The borderless policy of ECOWAS has, however, been challenged by several factors among which are socio-economic developments across member states leading to diverse reactions, hence altering the migration configurations of the sub-region.

The diversity of economic groupings with varied objectives, markets size, structure and membership also meant that different interests were being pursued by member states. At the same time, the wavering political support, political instability and inter-state border disputes among member states also affected the pact. For instance, the border disputes between Mauritania and Senegal, and Ghana and Togo, resulting in the expulsion of community citizens were in contradiction of the Protocol of Free Movement. The division of the sub-region along colonial heritage created a kind of supremacy battle among the Francophone and Anglophone countries. The persistent economic downturn facing member states affected their ability to pursue consistent macro-economic policies as well as the funding of cooperation unions. There is also the problem of arriving at common tariff regimes since there are about eight odd currencies in use in the sub-region, with the exception of CFA Franc which unites the francophone countries. There are rising rates of poverty and unemployment among member states, poor transport network with railways having different track systems and norms. Cross-border trade often assumes informal nature since it is often unrecorded due to corrupt practices among customs and immigration officials. Some member states sabotaged the free movement pact at various points in time. For instance, in 1999, Mauritania indicated to pull out of the group and withdrew her membership in June 2000. Cape Verde was on the verge of pulling out just before the coup d'état in that country, which changed the course of events. Also, in 2004, Liberia threatened to expel some foreign residents from member state's describing them as irregular migrants. Other challenges to the free movement pact include xenophobia in some countries, e.g., the activities of touts, corrupt customs and immigration officials in Cote d'Ivoire, who make travelling across borders difficult and expensive. In response to some of these challenges, especially those relating to issues on migration management, ECOWAS came up with some policies with the following objectives:

- Information and awareness campaigns for potential migrants on the dangers of irregular migration and smuggling networks;
- Cooperation between ECOWAS Member States with regard to controlling clandestine migration and dismantling the mafia-like networks;
- Cooperation between ECOWAS Member States in collaboration with host countries with a view to combating clandestine migration;
- Cooperation with host countries to provide logistics and funding for voluntarily returning migrants in transit countries and countries of origin;
- Affirmation of the principle of the return of clandestine migrants respecting their dignity and fundamental human rights;
- Implementation by ECOWAS Member States, of measures enabling the reinsertion of irregular migrants upon their return;
- Development of technical and financial cooperation with ECOWAS Member States in the area of managing emergency situations with regard to irregular migration;
- Compliance with international commitments made by Member States regarding migration (ECOWAS 2007).

However, to what extent these laudable objectives are attained has been the subject of much controversy. The current state of events still makes the ECOWAS Free movement pact, which is a core aspect of the regional integration, a far cry from what obtains in the European Union.

The Way Forward

The need to urgently review developments in the sub-region is essential if the much-talked-about integration is to be possible. To this end, a number of initiatives and resources will have to be put together by policy makers in the sub-region.

Information Sharing and Policing Cooperation

There is an absolute need for a regional approach to policing and information sharing. Attempts should be made to undertake cooperative research and information sharing between countries of origin and destination. It is also important for law enforcement agencies in destination countries to share information on socio-demographics of trafficked persons as well as smuggling routes with agencies in countries of origin. The extent of cooperation among terrorist groups in the continent coupled with the advantage of globalization requires that a regional approach be used in policing the migration of people. There is the need therefore, to reinforce joint patrols and establish a Joint Task Force to be known as ECOPOL with the main objective of granting national law enforcement authorities access to relevant information (such as DNA and fingerprint and other migrants' databases).

Checking the Excesses of Customs and Immigration Officials

Law enforcement agents at the points of entry and exit need to be given adequate enlightenment on the benefits of the integration plan as well as the bad image which corrupt practices can give to the region. However, this will require that such agents be well motivated and equipped for the task. Law enforcement agents should also be updated with modern techniques of combating innovative criminal acts like cybercrime, money laundering and other evolving trans-national crimes.

Involvement of Civil Society Groups

To ensure a reliable response to the challenges of migration across the sub-region, there is the need for a systemic approach by which governments at the national and regional levels will collaborate with civil society groups in managing the challenges of migration-related crimes across the sub-region. A very good example is in the area of controlling the menace of human trafficking, especially of women and children. Research has shown that victims of trafficking cooperate better with Non-Governmental Organizations (NGOs) than law enforcement agents in terms of rehabilitation and repatriation (Ikuteyijo 2013).

Promoting Good Governance

ECOWAS should also ensure that good governance is their hallmark in all member states. The peer review mechanism by which member states will set minimum benchmarks for heads of state in terms of delivering the dividends of governance to the citizens should be encouraged. This will checkmate possible abuse of power by incumbents and allow for a fair distribution of resources among the diverse conglomeration of ethnic and religious interests represented in the sub-region.

Monitoring and Evaluation of Policies

Since the creation of ECOWAS, there have been many laudable goals of the founding fathers which are yet to be implemented. Others were initiated but abandoned by successive administrations. There is therefore the need to have ways of monitoring and evaluating these policies so as to justify the human and financial resources expended in putting them together. This can be achieved by establishing research and documentation institutes in reputable universities in each member state.

Support of Cross-country Research

There should be more cutting-edge research efforts between researchers in origin and destination countries that focus on, for example, ethnographic studies of trafficked victims in order to have a more systemic perspective of the phenomenon. Above all, channels of communication between countries of destination and origin must be established and reinforced, and information sharing in form of research findings will form a major component of cooperation.

Infrastructural Development at Border Areas

Efforts should be made by relevant government agencies to strengthen the policy of provision of social amenities and infrastructure in border areas. This will be in the form of infrastructure like schools, hospitals, electricity and portable water, in order to gain the trust of the communities and secure their support for government policies.

Personal Identification and Migration Database

Lastly, there is the need to revamp the moribund national identification schemes of most member states to ensure that there is a database for the monitoring of citizens in the sub-region. Subsequently, the identification exercise will be extended to the regional level.

References

Addo, P., 2006, 'Cross-Border Criminal Activities in West Africa: options for Effective Responses', Kofi Annan International Peace Keeping Training Centre (KAIPTC) Paper No. 12, May.

Adepoju, A., 2005, 'Review of Research and Data on Human Trafficking in Sub-Saharan Africa', *International Migration*, Vol. 43 (1/2), pp. 75-93.

Adepoju, A., 2005, 'Review of Research and Data on Human Trafficking in Sub-Saharan Africa', *International Migration*, Vol. 43 (1/2), pp. 75-93.

Adepoju, A. and Van der Wiel, A., 2010, *Seeking Greener Pastures Abroad: A Migration Profile of Nigeria*, Ibadan, Safari Books Limited.

Adepoju, A., 2006, 'Leading Issues in International Migration in Sub-Saharan Africa', in *Views on Migration in Sub-Saharan Africa*, HSRC Press, Proceedings of an African Migration Alliance Workshop.

Anarfi, J.K., 2001, 'Ghanaian Women and Prostitution in Cote d'Ivoire', in K. Kempadoo and J. Doezema, eds, *Global Sex Workers: Rights, Resistance and Redefinition*, New York, Routlege.

Baldwin-Edwards, M., 2008, 'Towards a theory of illegal migration: historical and structural components', *Third World Quarterly* 29(7).

Berman, E.G., 2001, 'Arming the Revolutionary United Front', *African Security Review* 10, 1.

Cvajner, M. and Sciortino, G., 2010, 'Theorizing irregular migration: the control of spatial mobility in differentiated societies', *European Journal of Social Theory* 13.

Darkwa, L., 2011, *The Challenge of Sub-regional Security in West Africa: The Case of 2006 ECOWAS Convention on Small Arms and Light Weapons*, Uppsala, NordiskaAfrikaInstitutet.

De Genova, N., 2002, 'Migrant "illegality" and deportability in everyday life', *Annual Review of Anthropology* 31.

De Hass, H., 2007, *The Myth of Invasion*, International Migration Institute, Oxford University, http://www.iom.int.

De Haas, H., 2008, *Irregular Migration from West Africa to the Maghreb and the European Union: An Overview of Recent Trends*, Geneva, International Organization for Migration (IOM).

Donato, K.M. and Armenta, A., 2011, 'What do we know about undocumented migration?', *Annual Review of Sociology* 37.

ECOWAS Small Arms Control Programme (ECOSAP), 2010, Annual Report, http://www.ecosap.ecowas.int/index.php?option=com_jotloader&view=categories&cid=0_11910765ecb7da29da3ff7029b829ef0&Itemid=84&lang=en (accessed 16September 2011).

ECOWAS, 2007, Draft Report of the Meeting of Ministers on ECOWAS Common Approach to Migration, Abuja, Nigeria, 14th June.

Ehindero, S. and Idemudia, P., 2006, *Baseline Study on Forced Labour and Human Trafficking in Kwara, Kano, Cross Rivers and Lagos States in Nigeria*, Abuja, ILO/PATWA Offices in Nigeria, Ghana, Sierra Leone and Liberia.

Espenshade, T. J., 1995, 'Unauthorized immigration to the United States', *Annual Review of Sociology* 21, Fall 2005.

Fall, H., 2005, 'Border Controls and Cross-Border Crimes in West Africa', in *Combating the Proliferation of Small Arms and Light Weapons in West Africa: Handbook for the Training of Armed and Security Forces*, A. Aissi and I. Sall, eds, Geneva, Switzerland, United Nations' Institute for Disarmament Research (UNIDR).

Ghosh, B., 2000, 'Introduction: Towards a New International Regime for Orderly Movements of People', in B. Ghosh, ed., *Managing Migration – Time for a New International Regime?*, Oxford, Oxford University Press, pp. 6-26.

Goldin, Ian, Cameron, Geoffrey and Balarajan, Meera,2011, *Exceptional People: How Migration shaped our World and will define our Future*, Princeton University Press.

Guild, E., 2004, 'Who is an Irregular Migrant?' in B. Bogusz, ed., *Irregular Migration and Human Rights: Theoretical, European, and International Perspectives*, Leiden: MartinusNijhoff Publishers.

Guild, E., 2010, *Criminalization of Migration in Europe: Human Rights Implications,* Issue Paper, Council of Europe, Commissioner for Human Rights, Strasbourg.

Ikuteyijo, L.O., 2013, 'Patterns and Processes of Irregular Migration among Youths in Nigeria', Unpublished Ph.D. thesis submitted to the Department of Sociology and Anthropology, Obafemi Awolowo University, Ile-Ife, Nigeria.

International Labour Organization, 2003, 'The Trafficking of Women and Children in Southern African Region', Presentation of Research Findings, ILO, Geneva, 24 March.

International Labour Organization, 2009, *The Cost of Coercion*, Global Report under the Follow-up to the ILO Declaration on Fundamental Principles and Rights at Work. Geneva, ILO. www.ilo.org/declaration

Koser, Khalid, 2005, 'Irregular Migration, State Security and Human Security',*Global Commission on International Migration (GCIM),* Paper for the Policy Analysis and Research Programme of the Global Commission on International Migration.

Kubal, A., 2012, 'Conceptualizing Semi-legality in Migration Research', International Migration Institute Working Paper Series, Paper 58, University of Oxford.

Leighton, C., 2000, 'New efforts to free hostages in S Leone after release of Five', *Relief Web*, 31 August , http://reliefweb.int (accessed 20 April 2011)

Manian, Sabita, 2010, 'Sex Trafficking in the Horn of Africa', in *Sex Trafficking: A Global Perspective,* McCabe Kimberly and Manian Sabita, eds, United Kingdom, Lexington Books,pp. 13-24.

Massey, D.S., 2003, 'Patterns and Processes of International Migration in the 21st Century', Paper Prepared for the Conference on African migration in Contemporary Perspective, Johannesburg, South Africa, 4-7 June.

Ndime, D., 2005, 'Cooperation Between States to Combat the Proliferation of Small Arms and Light Weapons', in *Combating the Proliferation of Small Arms and Light Weapons in West Africa: Handbook for the Training of Armed and Security Forces,* A. Aissi and I. Sall, eds, United Nations' Institute for Disarmament Research (UNIDR) Geneva, Switzerland, pp. 77-84.

Portes, A., 1978, 'Toward a structural analysis of illegal (undocumented) immigration', *International Migration Review* 12(4).

Stan, R., 2006, 'Improving the Management of Migration: How to Decrease Irregular Migration, and Strengthen Confidence in the Ministry of Labour', A Policy paper of the Centre for Policy Studies, Budapest.

Taylor, E., 2002 'Trafficking in Women and Girls', Paper Presented for Group Meeting on trafficking in Women and Girls, Glen Cove, New York, 18-22 November.

Triandafyllidou, A., 2010, 'Irregular Migration in Europe in the Early 21st Century', in A. Triandafyllidou, ed., *Irregular Migration in Europe: Myths and Realities,* Fanham, Ashgate.

Trosper, T.B., 2009, 'West Africa's War on Terrorism: Time and Patience', An unpublished Masters of Research Degree / Strategic Research Project submitted to the U.S. Army War College, Pennsylvania.

United Nations International Children Educational Fund, (UNICEF), 2003, *United Kingdom Child Trafficking Information Sheet,* January.

United Nations Office of Drug and Crime (UNODC), 2009, *Anti-Human Trafficking Manual for Criminal JusticePractitioners.Vienna:*UNODC.www.unodc.org/unodc/en/human-trafficking/anti-human-trafficking-manual.html

World Bank, 2009, Social Development Notes: Conflict, Crime and Violence. No 122/December www.worldbank.org/EXTSOCIALDEVELOPMENT/RESOURCES? 244362/HumanTrafficking_pdf/

Yacubu, Y.G., 2005, 'Cooperation among Armed Forces and the Security Forces in Combating the Proliferation of Small Arms', in *Combating the Proliferation of Small Arms and Light Weapons in West Africa: Handbook for the Training of Armed and Security Forces,* A. Aissi and I. Sall, eds, Geneva, Switzerland, United Nations' Institute for Disarmament Research (UNIDR) pp. 55-69.

Printed in the United States
By Bookmasters